The Lamb is all the Glory

The Lamb
is all the
Glory

Richard Brooks

EVANGELICAL PRESS

EVANGELICAL PRESS
Faverdale North Industrial Estate, Darlington, DL3 0PH, England

Evangelical Press USA
P. O. Box 84, Auburn, MA 01501, USA

e-mail: sales@evangelicalpress.org

web: http://www.evangelicalpress.org

First published 1986
Second impression 2002

British Library Cataloguing in Publication Data available

ISBN 0 85234 229 2

Typeset by Inset, Chappel, Essex
Printed and bound in Great Britain by Creative Print & Design Wales,
Ebbw Vale

The sands of time are sinking;
    The dawn of heaven breaks;
The summer morn I've sighed for,
    The fair, sweet morn, awakes:
Dark, dark hath been the midnight,
    But dayspring is at hand,
And glory, glory dwelleth
    In Immanuel's land.

The King there, in His beauty,
    Without a veil is seen;
It were a well-spent journey,
    Though seven deaths lay between;
The Lamb with His fair army
    Doth on Mount Zion stand,
And glory, glory dwelleth
    In Immanuel's land.

O Christ, He is the fountain,
    The deep, sweet well of love;
The streams on earth I've tasted,
    More deep I'll drink above;
There, to an ocean fulness,
    His mercy doth expand,
And glory, glory dwelleth
    In Immanuel's land.

The bride eyes not her garment,
    But her dear bridegroom's face;
I will not gaze at glory,
    But on my King of grace;
Not on the crown He giveth,
    But on His piercèd hand:
THE LAMB IS ALL THE GLORY
    Of Immanuel's land.

                    Anne Ross Cousin
                    1824–1906

Contents

A word of introduction

The book of Revelation! It is always a joy and privilege to begin the study of any book of the Bible, but especially so when it is the book of Revelation. Maybe you are already familiar with the book, to a greater or lesser degree. But for some perhaps this is the first serious visit you have made to this often neglected portion of the Word of God.

At the outset, we would do well to remember two things: *the testimony of the apostle Paul* that *'All Scripture is God-breathed and is useful* for teaching, rebuking, correcting and training in righteousness, so that the man of God may be thoroughly equipped for every good work' (2 Timothy 3:16–17); and *the promise of the Lord Jesus Christ Himself* that 'When he, the Spirit of truth, comes, *he will guide you into all truth* . . . He will bring glory to me by taking from what is mine and making it known to you' (John 16:13–14). If 'all Scripture', then does that not include the book of Revelation? And if 'all truth', does that not do the same?

So let us not be frightened of what lies before us. Rather may God bless it to our souls. 'To him who loves us and has freed us from our sins by his blood . . . to him be glory and power for ever and ever! Amen' (1:5–6). Without further delay, and with our Bibles open before us (mine is the New International Version) let us come to consider the first chapter, making this our prayer:

Spirit of God, my Teacher be,
Showing the things of Christ to me.

7

Outline analysis of Revelation

Christ is all!   (1:1—20)
    Title and introduction (1—3)
    The glorious gospel of God (4—8)
    The glorious vision of Christ (9—18)
    The stars and the lampstands (19—20)

The letters to the seven churches of Asia   (2:1—3:22)
    Ephesus, the loveless church (2:1—7)
    Smyrna, the persecuted church (2:8—11)
    Pergamum, the compromising church (2:12—17)
    Thyatira, the over-tolerant church (2:18—29)
    Sardis, the dying church (3:1—6)
    Philadelphia, the church with opportunity (3:7—13)
    Laodicea, the lukewarm church (3:14—22)

The vision of heaven   (4:1—5:14)
    God in His majesty and holiness (4:1—11)
    Christ in His redeeming glory (5:1—14)

The seven seals   (6:1—8:1)
    1st seal (6:1—2)
    2nd seal (6:3—4)
    3rd seal (6:5—6)
    4th seal (6:7—8)
    5th seal (6:9—11)
    6th seal (6:12—17)

    Interlude: the sealing and security of God's elect (7:1—17)

    7th seal (8:1)

The seven trumpets   (8:1—11:19)
   Preparation (8:2—6)
   1st trumpet (8:7)
   2nd trumpet (8:8—9)
   3rd trumpet (8:10—11)
   4th trumpet (8:12—13)
   5th trumpet (9:1—12)
   6th trumpet (9:13—21)

   Interlude: The angel and the little scroll (10:1—11)
           The measuring rod (11:1—2)
           The two witnesses (11:3—14)

   7th trumpet (11:15—19)

The Lamb, the woman and the dragon   (12:1—14:20)
   The woman, the dragon and the man-child (12:1—6)
   War in heaven (12:7—12)
   War between Satan, the woman and her son (12:13—17)
   The beast out of the sea (13:1—10)
   The beast out of the earth (13:11—18)
   The Lamb and the elect upon Mount Zion (14:1—5)
   The three angels with their messages (14:6—13)
   The harvest of God's wrath (14:14—20)

The seven bowls   (15:1—16:21)
   Preparation (15:1—16:1)
   1st bowl (16:2)
   2nd bowl (16:3)
   3rd bowl (16:4—7)
   4th bowl (16:8—9)
   5th bowl (16:10—11)
   6th bowl (16:12—16)
   7th bowl (16:17—21)

The fall of Satan and the triumph of the Lamb   (17:1—20:15)
   The character and history of Babylon (17:1—18)
   The fall of Babylon (18:1—24)
   The wedding of the Lamb (19:1—10)
   The battle of Armageddon (19:11—21)
   The thousand years (20:1—10)
   The final judgement (20:11—15)

All things new! (21:1—22:5)
  A new heaven and a new earth (21:1—8)
  The holy city (21:9—27)
  Paradise restored (22:1—5)

The end of the Bible (22:6—21)
  A welcome reminder (22:6)
  A promised event (22:7—16, 20)
  A gracious invitation (22:17, 20)
  A fence around the Scriptures (22:18—19)
  The last word: grace (22:21)

1.
Christ is all!

Please read Revelation 1:1—18

The whole of the Bible is full of Christ. It testifies to Him. Whether you turn to the Old Testament or the New Testament, to the Law or the Prophets, to the Psalms or the Gospels, to the historical books or the epistles, 'These are the Scriptures that testify about me,' says Jesus (John 5:39). And this is gloriously so with the book of Revelation. John does not dominate the book. It is not his revelation. Everything focuses upon the One who is the Lord of glory — the Lord Jesus Christ. We can see that clearly from the very moment the book opens.

1. The beginning of the revelation (1:1—3)

The title of the book
First words, like last words, are always important. The very first words of this, the last book of the Bible, are those we usually take as its title: '**the revelation of Jesus Christ**'. The word translated 'revelation' is crucial. It means 'unveiling', and is used in Scripture of the uncovering of something that is hidden and, in particular, of the making known by God of what, left to himself, man would be permanently incapable of finding out. That gives us a vital clue to the nature and interpretation of this whole book. We are introduced here to amazing, wonderful and mysterious matters which our natural eyes cannot see, our natural ears cannot hear and our natural unaided minds and hearts cannot begin to understand or appreciate.

But it is not just any revelation, but 'the revelation of

13

Jesus Christ'. We should take 'of' in the sense of 'about'
or 'concerning', and this gives us a second vital clue about
the book. It reveals the Lord Jesus Christ to us. Indeed it
does — in all His glory as the sinner's Saviour (1:5), the
eternal God (1:8), the Conqueror of death and Hades who
is alive for ever and ever (1:18), the glorious Head of the
church who dwells and walks in the midst of his people
(2:1), the Overcomer of all His enemies and the One through
whom all believers are victorious (17:14), the One who
invites us to His marriage supper (19:9) and the glorious
Coming One (1:7; 22:20). How that should whet our
spiritual appetites!

The communication of the book

God is the Author of the book of Revelation, as He is of
the whole of Scripture. That is, God in His triune glory
and splendour, not just the First Person of the Trinity.
But it is still correct to speak of God 'giving' the revelation
'to' the Son, for God is described elsewhere as 'the God and
Father of our Lord Jesus Christ' (1 Peter 1:3). Christ then,
in His turn, **'made it known'** (literally 'signified it', for the
book is full of visions, signs and symbols, which is what
makes it at first glance less straightforward than some other
parts of the Bible) by **'his angel'** (for the angels are Christ's
messengers who do His bidding) **'to his servant John'**.

By John we understand 'the disciple whom Jesus loved'
(John 13:23), he who leaned on Jesus' bosom at the Last
Supper and who penned the Gospel and the three epistles
which bear his name. Before Christ called John to be a
disciple he had been a fisherman on the Sea of Galilee with
his father and brother. During his years as a disciple he had
been privileged, along with Peter and James, to share and
witness those intimate moments with the Saviour in the
home of Jairus, on the mount of transfiguration and in the
Garden of Gethsemane. He had been at the foot of the cross
when Jesus died at Calvary and one of the first at the tomb
from which Jesus had risen. This is the traditional view of
authorship and there are no persuasive reasons for changing
it. And John, in his turn, **'testifies to everything he saw'**,
writing it down.

How we can rejoice, therefore, at the security of the

transmission and formation of Scripture! We have indeed 'the word of God and the testimony of Jesus Christ' — and that word and testimony are sure and true.

The blessing of the book

There is great encouragement arising from verse 3. Blessing is promised for those who 'read . . . hear . . . and take to heart' the words of the book. What a mouth-watering incentive to carry our study on through to the end!

But mark well that ascending scale. We must not only read (eyes) and hear (ears), but take to heart the Word of God (cf. Psalm 119:11; Colossians 3:16), and this must lead to the response of personal, practical submission and obedience (James 1:22).

Surely among the blessings in store are a greater prizing and appreciation of the Lord Jesus Christ as He is set before us as our all-in-all, a greater encouragement to faith in Him and a more realistic and informed view of all that is going on around us in history and current affairs. For we must learn to see everything (whether it be wars, nuclear threats, economic collapse, personal trials, the persecution of believers, or whatever) in the perspective that the book of Revelation gives us. All things will and must lead to the final manifestation of Christ in His glory. The song of 11:15 will be sung: 'The kingdom of the world has become the kingdom of our Lord and of his Christ, and he will reign for ever and ever.' With regard to all this, 'the time is near', with which we need to compare the statement in verse 1: 'what must soon take place'. That does not mean that the book is to be to us a pocket calculator or that we should start predicting dates. Together these two remarks remind us that in the first instance the message of Revelation was addressed to the believers of John's own day; but they also speak of the constant relevance of the book and the fact that all things are hastening to the end. But remember that God's measure of time is very different from our own (2 Peter 3:8–10).

2. Glorious gospel and glorious Saviour (1:4–18)

This great section of chapter 1 focuses first upon the glorious

gospel of God (4—8) and then upon the glorious vision of
Christ (9—18), but before considering these themes let us
gather up the details furnished in verse 4 and verses 9—10
with regard to the revelation itself.

We have already spoken of John and who he is, but now
we learn also where he was when he received the revelation
('**on the island of Patmos**'), why he was there ('**because of
the word of God and the testimony of Jesus**'), what day of
the week it was ('**the Lord's Day**' — when better?), what
condition he was in ('**in the Spirit**') and to whom the
revelation was to be delivered ('**the seven churches in the
province of Asia**' that are then named). Each of these details
is important and together they heighten the reality of all
that happened.

Patmos was an island in the Aegean Sea, roughly four miles
by eight miles, and a desolate, uninviting and inhospitable
place of mountains and marble quarries. John had no
Christian fellowship there, having been removed at a great
age from the church at Ephesus, yet the very wilderness of
his exile proved for him to be the gate of heaven. Things
are not always as they seem!

> Ye fearful saints, fresh courage take,
> The clouds ye so much dread
> Are big with mercy, and shall break
> In blessings on your head.

The whole of that fine hymn by William Cowper, beginning with the line 'God moves in a mysterious way', is
worthy of careful meditation in this connection.

It was around the year A.D. 96 and the Roman Emperor
Domitian hated the sight and sound of the gospel and was
sorely persecuting the church of Christ. Hence John's banish-
ment for gospel faithfulness. As his thoughts went back to
his beloved flock, from whom he was now separated, see
how warmly he describes himself as '**your brother and
companion in the suffering and kingdom and patient endurance that are ours in Jesus**'. What a powerful triad is
there! Suffering, in one form or another and to one degree
or another, is a 'given' for the Christian, and this will call
for great patience and endurance. But another 'given' is the

kingdom of the Lord Jesus Christ, which no one can take away from Him and no one can take from His people. The young, greatly afflicted believer James Laing once remarked, 'Five minutes in glory will make up for all this suffering.'[1]

On the Lord's Day (the first day of the week, the day of resurrection) John was 'in the Spirit'. What does that mean? 'He sees, indeed, but not with physical eyes. He hears, but not with physical ears. He is in direct spiritual contact with his Saviour. He is alone . . . with God! He is wide awake and every avenue of his soul is wide open to the direct communication coming from God,' writes William Hendriksen.[2] William Still observes that he was 'taken over by the Spirit and elevated . . . to a high degree of spiritual sensitivity and reception, which led to divine insight into the holy mysteries of God'.[3] What he received he was commanded to write and send to the churches, just as Paul the apostle wrote, in the first instance, to particular churches. We shall look at those churches individually later on.

The glorious gospel of God
A magnificent contemporary hymn by W. Vernon Higham begins: 'Great is the gospel of our glorious God,' and that should be our own feeling upon the matter as we consider the picture of the gospel given here.

It originates in grace and issues in peace (4). The gospel is the gospel of grace from start to finish. Grace is the love, mercy and favour of God to sinners – those who not only do not deserve it but actually and positively deserve the exact opposite – His wrath and condemnation. And grace is not done with at conversion. We continue in utter dependence upon it all our days. Peace has been described by Matthew Henry in his famous commentary as 'the sweet evidence and assurance of His grace', and by Dr Hendriksen as 'the reflection of the smile of God in the heart of the believer who has been reconciled to God through the Lord Jesus Christ'. It follows grace. The two are mentioned side by side on various occasions in the Bible (cf. Romans 5:1–2).

It derives from the Godhead (4–5). Each of the three Persons of the Godhead is involved in our salvation and they are mentioned here in the order Father, Spirit, Son. The phrase 'the seven spirits' is a familiar designation for the Holy Spirit in the book of Revelation, pointing to the fulness of His work and the variety of His operations. If you should be wondering why the order of the Persons of the Godhead is not the usual one, then the reason ordinarily given (and probably the correct one) is that John's vision will involve him looking, or peeping, into heaven itself. Now the Jewish tabernacle was 'a copy and shadow of what is in heaven' (Hebrews 8:5), and in that tabernacle the ark in the Holy of Holies represented the throne of God, the lampstand with the seven branches in front of the ark represented the Spirit, while the altar, whose priests and sacrifices pointed to the Lord Jesus Christ, was in the courtyard in front of the Holy Place.

Two grand descriptions of God are given. In verse 4 He is the One 'who is, and who was, and who is to come', which is a reminder of His eternal self-existence. He was never created, nor will He ever end. And in verse 8 He Himself speaks and says, 'I am the Alpha and the Omega.' One writer likens this verse to 'the publisher's imprint at the bottom of the title page of a book'.[4] Alpha and Omega are the first and last letters of the Greek alphabet. In a book which treats of the great span of God's dealings down the ages, as Revelation does, this title is particularly appropriate for the God who is the beginning and the end of history and rules and controls all things according to the counsel of His own will. The application of the same title to Christ in 22:13 is yet another Scripture affirmation of His deity.

It focuses upon the Lord Jesus Christ (5—6). Three titles are given to Christ in verse 5. He is 'the faithful witness', manifesting God with a reliable and true testimony at all times. He is 'the firstborn from the dead', for not only has He been raised from the dead, but by that same power we too shall be raised up. Compare Paul's great argument on this very point in 1 Corinthians 15:20—28. And He is 'the ruler of the kings of the earth', for He is 'King of kings and Lord of lords' (19:16), and all earthly kings receive their authority from Him and are accountable to Him. As verse 6

continues we find how utterly indebted we are to Christ
and how absolutely complete in Him we are — loved,
washed, freed from sin and guilt. He has turned us into
kings in His royal kingdom, for we reign in life through
Christ (Romans 5:17), and how much more so when we
shall be in glory with Him! And He has given us the
character of priests, which speaks of our access to the
Father through Him, our prevailing power in prayer
because of Him and the spiritual worship of our lips and
our lives which we are to bring to Him.

It looks forward to His coming again (7). History is not
just drifting aimlessly along. Everything is moving
deliberately and irrevocably towards the return of Christ,
an event He often spoke of Himself in the Gospels. There
will be no doubt about it when it comes — it will be a
decisive, supernatural event for all to see. And it will affect
all people, for He comes to gather His people to Himself,
but to judge those who have rejected Him. The Old Testament background to this verse includes Zechariah 12:10.
That rich prophetic announcement had a poignant fulfilment at the crucifixion (John 19:37), when the Jews literally
pierced the Son of God in His human nature. They did that
out of malice and hatred, though in God's saving grace at
Pentecost some cast a saving look upon Him and experienced
true repentance. But Zechariah's prophecy looks on further
than that as well — even to the coming of the Lord Jesus
Christ in glory to judge the world. But the mourning of
those who have pierced Him will then be very different,
for the mourning of verse 7 is a mourning of anguish, misery
and wasted opportunity, not of repentance. Repentance
has been left too late. How 'the eye of saint and sinner
[should] be fixed more steadily and believingly on this
coming day of wrath and terror to every impenitent soul
and of glory and perfected bliss to every child of God'![5]
Scripture is always the best expounder of Scripture, so have
a look at 2 Thessalonians 1:6—10 for a fuller commentary
upon this.

The glorious vision of Christ
You cannot get away from the 'Christ is all!' theme! John

heard behind him 'a loud voice like a trumpet' — remember
how in the Old Testament the people would often be
gathered together by the blowing of a trumpet in order to
hear what God had to say to them. He turned around and
the Mediterranean sights that he had been getting used to
in his exile began to fade and instead what immediately met
his gaze and increasingly ravished his sight was a most
glorious view of the Lord Jesus Christ Himself! Christ was
walking among seven golden lampstands, which, as we shall
see, represent the seven churches already mentioned, and
which, in turn, are representative of the whole church of
Christ throughout history. John's eyes fell upon one aspect
of Christ's glory after another and the overwhelming and
overpowering effect of the whole view is described in
verse 17: 'When I saw him, I fell at his feet as though dead.'
It is most significant that the first chapter of the book
begins in this way, for what we need at all times — and most
especially in times which call for particular endurance — is a
view of the Lord Jesus Christ as He is. There is profound
truth in the old familiar lines:

> Turn your eyes upon Jesus,
> Look full in His wonderful face;
> And the things of earth will grow strangely dim
> In the light of His glory and grace
> > (H. H. Lemmel).

To analyse the different elements of the vision is to run
into the danger of losing that total picture and effect which
so struck John. So we shall not pry too closely — and before
doing anything else at all read through verses 12—16 several
times and meditate upon those verses. What did John see?

v. 13. The expression 'like a son of man' (cf. Daniel 7:
13—14 and Jesus' own use of the title) speaks of the real
manhood and humanness of Christ, sympathizing, tempted
as we are (though without sin), and touched with a feeling
of our infirmities. But He is no longer the humiliated and
suffering servant but the glorified Lord, having received a
kingdom and an everlasting dominion from the Father.
The robe and sash speak of His high-priestly character both

past and present — the finished sacrificial work at Calvary along with the present intercessory ministry in glory.

v. 14. The whiteness declares the eternity and divinity and purity of the One who is the Ancient of Days. He does not decay, grow old or lose His power. And the eyes set forth His heart-searching omniscience — you know the power of a gaze, but no one has a gaze like Jesus!

v. 15. The feet represent what someone has called His 'resistless providence', as He works out all His purposes, treads down all His enemies and executes all His judgements. The voice is of the God who makes Himself heard in words of salvation and comfort, of warning and judgement. In comparison, the sound of Niagara Falls is small fry!

v. 16. We shall come to the stars a little later. The sword is the symbol of His authority and power to teach and judge, and the fact that it is sharp and double-edged shows that He cannot be avoided. And the final note of the verse displays the Holy One, too intense for sinful human eyes to behold! Christ's absolute perfection is the keynote all the way through.

As we prostrate ourselves with the apostle John, so we cry out, 'Hallelujah! What a Saviour!' Oh, for a grander, more glorious view of the Lord Jesus Christ in our own day and in our own life and worship — more raptures of joy in His presence and more awesome, trembling, godly fear before Him! Do we really know what it is to be 'lost in wonder, love and praise'?

Christ's words to John in verses 17–18 provide a wonderful application of the vision he has just received. For seeing who Christ is, knowing that 'The Son is the radiance of God's glory and the exact representation of his being' (Hebrews 1:3), how can we stand before Him? How could such glory as this ever bring itself into any association or union with a sinful wretch like me? So Christ, graciously placing His hand upon John, directs him afresh to Calvary and the empty tomb. Christ is the divine Son of God ('**I am the First and the Last**') who, having become man for us, died in our place for our sins ('I was dead') and rose again ('behold I am alive for ever and ever!'). The glorious result is that our sins are forgiven, death no longer has dominion over us and the terrors of hell are vanquished ('I hold the keys of death and Hades').

He controls when we die and how we die and He has been through death for us. The keys in Christ's possession underscore this. Just as a gaoler with his bunch of keys locks or opens the prison door (you don't, if you're the prisoner!), so the Lord Jesus Christ has this mighty unlocking power over sin, death and the grave. This was intended to drive out John's fears, and nothing less can do the same with ours. Here is good news for living and good news for dying! Nothing 'will be able to separate us from the love of God that is in Christ Jesus our Lord' (Romans 8:39).

Christ is all!

2.
The Christ of the church and the church of Christ

Please read Revelation 1:19—3:22

The book of Revelation is timeless. That is the chief principle to get hold of in this section. Here we meet the seven churches which have already been mentioned in Christ's instruction to John back in 1:11. In this chapter I shall lay down certain ground rules for interpreting chapters 2 and 3 of Revelation, in order afterwards to expound the letters to the churches one by one. But before all that we must pick up some vital information from 1:19—20.

1. The stars and the lampstands

The apostle John is told to 'write . . . **what you have seen, what is now and what will take place later**'. That statement itself confirms that the message of this last book of the Bible is for all time. It is not limited to any one particular age of world or church history. But what is meant by the stars and lampstands, and why are they such important symbols?

The lampstands
Taking the lampstands first ('lampstands' is a better translation than 'candlesticks'), they represent the seven churches. It is an appropriate symbol, for the church, being the corporate fellowship of the people of God, is to be the light of the world, shining and witnessing for Christ who is Himself *the* light of the world. If the church is not doing this it is not being the church. Do you remember the apostle Paul's vivid call to the Philippian Christians to be 'children of

23

God without fault in a crooked and depraved generation, in which you shine like stars in the universe as you hold out the word of life'? (Philippians 2:15–16.)

It is not the church's business to make truth, alter truth or improve truth, but rather to receive it, stand firm upon it, contend earnestly for it, preach it, adorn it with holy living, and — if necessary — die for it.

That the lampstands are golden sets forth the lovely truth of the preciousness to Christ of His church, which He purchased with His own blood, not to mention the dazzling purity and holiness He desires to see in us.

The stars

And the stars? They are 'the angels of the seven churches', which only leads to the further question, what or who are the angels? They are not on this occasion to be taken as heavenly beings but as the ministers (pastors, elders, overseers) of the different local churches. If they are to be identified as real angels (the guardian angels of each church, as some have suggested), it is difficult to make sense of how you write a letter to an angelic being and how that letter could end up being read out to a congregation. And the proposal that the 'spirit' (prevailing ethos or character) of each church is meant is also difficult to accept for the same reasons. It is far clearer to take them as addressed to those whose responsibility before God and men was to give themselves to preaching, teaching, pastoring and ruling in the local churches, and this would have made the best sense for the original Christians who were in those churches. Each of the seven letters begins with 'To the angel of the church in . . . write'.

Christ — and the stars and lampstands

It is of great significance that the stars are *in* Christ's right hand and that He walks *among* the lampstands. Taking that second truth first, that the Lord Jesus Christ actually walks among (in the midst of) His church is a shattering truth which should make us thrill and tremble all at once. Yet this is one of the most exalted keynotes of the whole book — the living, glorious Lord Jesus Christ present in His church, however small, despised or persecuted the church may be.

It is obviously a spiritual and invisible presence, but it is no less real for that!

We learn from this that the church is Christ's own church. He is the Head and the church is His possession. The church is 'His body, the fulness of him who fills everything in every way' (Ephesians 1:23). We are accustomed to speak affectionately of 'our church', or when we have a particular pastor in mind may say, 'We go to so-and-so's church.' But the church is Christ's church. He is our Ruler and we are His own special people, loved from eternity, chosen in Him even before the creation of the world. We are the bride being prepared for Christ, our heavenly Bridegroom (plenty more on that later in the book!). We are a people under His authority and who should be characterized in our individual life, family life, church life, work life and, indeed, in all our relationships, by doing His will to His glory.

Caught up here also is the truth that Christ has absolute rights over us, to deal with His church as He will. This becomes evident very practically as the letters to the churches unfold, and as Christ there commends whatever He finds that pleases Him, rebukes the sins and weaknesses of His people, calls us to repentance and even, where extreme measures are called for, threatens us with His judgement and the removal of His life-giving presence. How carefully we need to heed the sevenfold refrain: 'He who has an ear, let him hear what the Spirit says to the churches.' And Christ walking among the lampstands speaks of His constant supervision of us, His eyes always upon us and His ears always listening to what we say (not just in the worship services and at the prayer meetings, but at the church business meetings as well!).

The stars are symbolically represented as being in Christ's right hand and this teaches us a collection of lessons we can only summarize here. His ministers must be called, equipped and sent by Him and be under His sway, or they have not been sent at all (Jeremiah 23:21). Their responsibility is to Him, for they keep watch over the flock of their charge 'as men who must give an account' (Hebrews 13:17). Respect and honour are due to the true ministers of Christ's gospel, for they are His under-shepherds (1 Timothy 5:17; 1 Thessalonians 5:12–13). And it is their business to preach

Christ, to hold Him up before the people and to be so out
of the picture themselves that nothing shall be seen but Him
(1 Corinthians 2:1—5). Do you love, pray for and generously
provide for your pastor as you should? Are your love and
devotion towards Christ plainly seen in the way you treat
and regard His servant?

Andrew Bonar, speaking of Robert Murray M'Cheyne,
remarked, 'All who knew him not only saw in him a burning
and a shining light, but felt also the breathing of the hidden
life of God.' A word to fellow ministers: oh, to be an
imitator of M'Cheyne as he was of Christ!

2. Ground rules for interpreting the letters to the churches

There are four of these which are especially important.

They are written to seven real churches
The churches named first of all in 1:11 and then individually
addressed by the Head of the church in chapters 2 and 3
are real churches in existence in different parts of Asia Minor
(which we would now call Turkey) in the first century A.D.
That may seem obvious, but it is important because some
have suggested that the whole business of the seven churches
is just a literary device. I would object most strongly to
this and insist that they were real churches, each composed
of real live Christians, who experienced joys and sorrows,
successes and failures, advances and setbacks just like our
own. The Saviour knew them all. They were not the only
churches, but were the ones personally selected by Christ
for His letters. No doubt the book of Revelation as a whole
was circulated to them all, so that they would be aware of
what Christ said to the other churches as well as what He
said to them.

How important the local church is! How seriously we
ought to take our belonging to it and our responsibilities
towards it! We can treat the matter of church membership
far too lightly, either never joining and giving ourselves
whole-heartedly at all, or else joining, resigning, joining
another fellowship and resigning and so on at our whim. The
One whose church it is disapproves greatly of such light-
hearted behaviour.

The churches, between them, are representative of the church of Christ at all times

In other words, Christ has written these letters to us as well as to them! The outline analysis given at the beginning of our study indicates that each church had a particular characteristic (some good, some bad) and these features add up to a picture of the ups and downs of the church of Christ throughout the ages: lack of love to Christ, faithfully facing persecution for His sake, falling into compromise rather than standing firm, indulging in over-tolerance at the expense of church discipline, preening itself that everything is just right when there is only empty form with no vital life and power, presented with great opportunities for evangelism and service, and growing lukewarm in devotion and duty. What a magnificently comprehensive, even if not exhaustive, picture!

And herein lies the book's timelessness. There is a message here for the church and the individual Christian in every age. And that these are the seven particular characteristics that Christ singles out for attention shows just how seriously we need to take them.

Why seven? Because that number stands for divine completeness or fulness. These are letters to the whole church.

There are abiding spiritual lessons to be learned for the church of Christ

It is not particularly helpful to spend too much time reviewing all the different schools of interpretation of Revelation, for an alarming number of fancies and speculations have been advanced down the years.[6] But a few remarks are worth making in order to underscore further the fact that the book as a whole and the letters in particular are teeming with spiritual lessons which have a constant application. For some have erred in thinking that the only purpose of Revelation was to pass on a message to the first-century churches and that there it finished — job done! But if so, why has it been included in Scripture? In that case it would have no value for generations after that first one.

Others have ingeniously carved up the whole period of church history into seven periods or ages and insist that each

of the seven letters refers to one of these. So a chronological sequence is imposed quite wrongly upon the letters.
For the sake of curiosity and to expose the folly of such
an approach, here is one typical scheme.[7]

Ephesus: the apostolic church of the first century, at first
flourishing but then beginning to flag in zeal;
Smyrna: the persecuted church under the later Roman
emperors up until the time of Constantine, who early in the
fourth century declared Christianity the 'official' religion;
Pergamum: the church from the time of Constantine's
public patronage to the rise of the papacy in the fourth and
fifth centuries;
Thyatira: the church from the rise of the papacy to the
Reformation in the fifteenth and sixteenth centuries;
Sardis: the post-Reformation church lapsing into deadness
during the sixteenth and seventeenth centuries;
Philadelphia: the days of evangelical revival and further
reformation in the eighteenth and nineteenth centuries, with
the development of great missionary movements;
Laodicea: the lukewarmness in the professing church of
our own day, which is to continue until Christ's return.

Let it be understood that that is only one of many
variations on this theme. One person's interpretation makes
the dead church at Sardis refer to the glorious age of the
Reformation! This whole system of interpretation is to be
rejected wholesale. If it were true, then — quite apart from
other problems it would create — it would severely limit
the value of the book for the original first-century
congregations.

The truth of the matter is this: the book of Revelation,
just like the letters of the apostle Paul, was at first directed
very specifically and searchingly to particular named
churches. But the Head of the church is also laying down
abiding spiritual principles and lessons, teaching eternal
truths and pressing undying applications for His church
throughout the whole of the gospel age until His return
from heaven in glory. The golden thread running through
the book — Christ's war with Satan, played out in the contest
between the church and the world — settles this. This is in

harmony with the whole of Scripture, where every part of God's revelation — whether Old Testament prophecy or New Testament epistle — is given in view of definite and contemporary local circumstances, but brings out truths of eternal significance.

There is a clear structure to the letters
If you look now at the letters themselves you will see this emerging quite naturally without in any way trying to impose a pattern:
1.   An address to the pastor of the church.
2.   A reference to some attribute of Christ that has been mentioned in John's vision of Him in chapter 1 (for example, compare 2:1 with 1:13, 16; 2:8 with 1:17—18; 2:12 with 1:16 and so on). So there is an intimate relationship between the vision of Christ and the letters from Christ, in order that we do not miss exactly who it is who is speaking to His church.
3.   A word of praise from Christ (except for Laodicea).
4.   A word of criticism from Christ (except for Smyrna and Philadelphia).
5.   A word of warning from Christ, expressed with such vividness that it is as if He were right at hand and ready there and then to come and deal with them.
6.   A word of exhortation from Christ to hear His word.
7.   A word of promise from Christ (the promises with which the letters end provide some of the richest and most precious promises to be found anywhere in the Word of God!).

Before we actually come to the great task of expounding these letters, you will see that, of the seven letters, Ephesus, Pergamum and Thyatira receive intermingled words of praise and rebuke from Christ; Sardis and Laodicea receive a decided rebuke, and Smyrna and Philadelphia receive unqualified praise.

Would you like to know in more detail what Christ thinks of His church and what He requires of us? Then read on!

3.
From Ephesus to Thyatira

Please read Revelation 2

The first four letters from Christ to the churches are recorded in chapter 2, beginning with Ephesus.

1. Ephesus: 'You have forsaken your first love' (2:1—7)

In external matters Ephesus was the most favoured and prosperous of all the seven churches of Asia. As a city it was the largest in the Roman province, the number one city in Asia, which gave it an obvious political importance. Its position as a seaport and a lively centre of trade routes gave it considerable commercial importance. And it was also, in the widest sense, a religious centre, for the temple of Diana was there, considered to be one of the wonders of the world (Acts 17:23—28), along with every form of paganism you could think of and a flourishing magical arts business.

Yet what a lovely thing that God had established a church there in the midst of such darkness, vice and unbelief! For Ephesus desperately needed the gospel. The apostle Paul had founded the church and laboured there for three years. Timothy had ministered there and so had the apostle John. Perhaps his pulse quickened noticeably as the Lord Jesus Christ chose to address Ephesus first of all, for John's heart was certainly there!

Jesus' commendation
The Lord Jesus Christ is very gracious (Hebrews 6:10). He is not slow to praise, comfort and encourage. He gives credit where it is due. And in the things here that He commended

are to be discerned some of the vital marks of a true evangelical church. The Christians at Ephesus demonstrated *whole-hearted commitment to the Lord's work* (2a), a church bustling with spiritual activity, everyone labourers together with God. They were *sound in doctrine and faithful in discipline* (2b, 6), both notes that need to be struck with fresh vigour in our day. The church of Christ must hold firm to the truth of Christ, the truth of the Word of God, for the church is 'the pillar and foundation of the truth' (1 Timothy 3:15). False claims must be dealt with and false teachers exposed. These Nicolaitans urged a lifestyle of sexual freedom and carnal satisfaction. They were nothing to do with Nicolas of Antioch, the deacon (Acts 6:5). And they were *ready to endure hardship for Christ* (3). They knew the costliness of discipleship — the daily denying of self, taking up the cross and following Jesus in a world that is hostile to Him and so very often hostile to those who are His. They did not flinch, flag or faint.

And so we might say, 'What a church!' Surely they had everything you could possibly desire in a church. But . . .

Jesus' condemnation
In His character as the One who 'walks among the seven golden lampstands', the Lord Jesus Christ saw something which troubled Him so much that He said, 'I hold this against you' (4). The implication is that this one thing had escaped the pastor's notice and had escaped the church members' notice, but it did not escape Christ's notice, for nothing ever does. And what was the trouble? Loss of first love to Christ. Loss of love towards the brethren is also included in Christ's censure. But this is invariably a symptom of the greater trouble — lack of love to Christ — just as a warm, vital and spontaneous love for the brethren in a local congregation flows out naturally from a vigorous love to Christ and a healthy sense of the love of God in and through Christ.

There is a searching lesson here. A church may be well established, even large and prosperous. It may be exhibiting all the grand features to which Christ has already drawn attention in Ephesus. Yet all the time a secret defect may silently but surely be eating away at the church and threatening its very existence. For the Lord Jesus Christ will not accept any one thing or any collection of things as a substitute for love to Himself. The reference to 'first love' reminds us of Jeremiah 2:2 — the warm, glowing, passionate love of youth. It is so easy in the Christ-believer relationship, as in the human marriage relationship, for love to 'settle in', to be taken for granted, or even to be replaced by bald duty. It was no longer first love to Christ which drove the Christians at Ephesus. Plenty of things were going on. In a real sense the work was getting done, and no doubt the notices for the week revealed a packed programme. But first love to Christ was no longer the throbbing life-blood of the church.

How is it with you? And how is it with your church? Are you in love with Jesus? What drives you?

Octavius Winslow traces several characteristics of declining love so that we may identify them and deal with them.[8] They include the following:

1. God becoming less an object of fervent desire, holy delight and frequent contemplation.

2. Loss of that sweet confidence and simple trust of a child before God.

3. Hard thoughts of God in some of His dealings.

4. Duty rather than privilege in spiritual exercises.

5. A less tender walk with God (that is to say, less trembling at the thought of offending Him, and so lighter views of sin).

6. Christ becoming less glorious to the eye and less precious to the heart.

7. Love to Christ's people starting to decay.

8. Our interest in the advancement and prosperity of Christ's cause beginning to wane.

Let us use this as a check-list for self-examination. And remember Proverbs 27:6: 'Faithful are the wounds of a friend' (AV). What a wonderful Friend we have in Jesus — but what a false friend He would be if He never told us of the sins He can see in our lives!

Jesus' counsel

The Master Physician not only pointed to the problem, but also set out the remedy. It can be summed up in three

words: remember, repent, return! (5). Decline of love to the
Lord Jesus is to be seen as a fall from a great height. Do we
see it that way? Remember how things were and compare
them with how things are now. And the summons to repent
further urges that we should view this forsaking of first love
as sin; so we must confess it as such before Him, that it
might be forgiven and blotted out and that we should know
once more the sweet and powerful influences of the Holy
Spirit melting, warming and reviving our hearts. Christ
desired that the whole life of the church (worship, preaching, pastoring, fellowship, evangelism, prayer, giving,
business) should spring once more from the healthy and
vital root of true love. In effect, He calls His church to
fall in love with Him all over again!

Jesus' persuasives

He adds a warning (5) and a promise (7). The warning is
no empty one, for Christ can perform what He says. And
in due time He did, and the church at Ephesus eventually
disappeared. A church cannot continue for ever on a loveless course. We see signs of this all around, where godly
ministries have been withdrawn, gospel fruitfulness brought
to an end and churches closed down or sold. We must each
look to ourselves.

But what a promise! It is a picture of the loveliness,
delight and intimacy which believers will have with the
Saviour in glory — a paradise far, far more glorious than
the one Adam lost, and a fellowship far, far more wonderful and thrilling. Then we shall prove that 'In thy presence
is fulness of joy' and 'At thy right hand there are pleasures
for evermore' (Psalm 16:11, AV).

2. Smyrna: 'Be faithful, even to the point of death' (2:8—11)

Smyrna, now called Izmir, was on the west coast of Asia
Minor and famous for its monetary system, schools of
medicine and science, broad street and a great open-air
theatre which seated twenty thousand people. Indeed it was
something of a rival to Ephesus for the title and reputation
of 'first city'.

The church receives no word of complaint from its Head here — not that they were perfect or that there was no room for improvement, for there always is! Christ's concern is to give them a challenge and an encouragement that it is possible as an individual Christian and as a church to live to please Christ, to receive His 'well done' and not to have to be upbraided constantly by Him. 'The faithful church in Smyrna receives the shortest letter and the warmest praise.'[9] It was probably founded by Paul during his third missionary journey, A.D. 53—56 (cf. Acts 19:10).

The call to be faithful
This was not a new characteristic that the Christians at Smyrna were to adopt. Rather they were to go on in the same way they were already evidencing. There will never be any moment in our lives on earth when we can afford to stop being faithful. It is an abiding duty. We are to be faithful in guarding and proclaiming the truth of the gospel entrusted to us by God, faithful in manifesting the spirit of Christ (not least to our enemies) and faithful in pressing on in the work that He has set our hands and hearts to, so that we may reap and not faint.

In seeking to live in this way the brethren faced afflictions, poverty and slander (9). The word for 'afflictions' means being opposed, hard pressed and in narrow straits. There were those among their opponents who were doing their best to squeeze them out of existence in the city. They were probably quite poor people even to begin with, but matters were made worse because Christians at this time were often thrown out of their employment and cut off like lepers from social activities, and so could be in real difficulty when it came to providing for their families and supporting their pastor. And look where the slander came from — those who prided themselves on their religiousness, but whom the Lord Jesus Christ designates 'a synagogue of Satan'!

Things were likely to hot up even further, for we see reference made to coming imprisonment and even to the possibility of being put to death (10).[10] The reference to 'persecution for ten days' is not a literal week and a half, but an assurance that it will be for a limited period — it will come to an end.

Again, though, we see Christ as the encourager of His people. How He builds them up with His double assurance that 'I know' (9), and His reminder of their true condition — 'yet you are rich!' John Newton writes,

> Solid joys and lasting treasure
> None but Zion's children know.

The precious promises
Christ gives a twofold promise in verses 10—11. 'I will give you the crown of life' is an appropriate promise for the folk at Smyrna, and especially so in connection with Christ's description of Himself to them in verse 8 as 'the First and the Last, who died and came to life again'. This promise of the crown of life (elsewhere called the crown of gold, or righteousness, or glory) speaks of the victor's place of honour in the new creation. What a glorious contrast: 'Be faithful, even to the point of death [that is, even though it may cost you your life] and I will give you the crown of life'!

And it is underscored by the second promise in verse 11b. The first death is physical death (the separation of body and soul at the end of our present life), and this, of course, is something that Christians are not exempt from. Indeed, it is something we may even have to meet violently, as many in the seven churches did, and so have many of the Lord's servants down the ages since and right up to our own day. But the second death (absolute separation for ever from the God who is the Fountain of life, joy and everything that is lovely and desirable) cannot touch or hurt the Christian. Why? We are secure in our crucified and risen Lord Jesus Christ! It is the doctrine of our union with Christ!

Let Anne Ross Cousin close this section for us:

> For me, Lord Jesus, Thou hast died,
> And I have died in Thee:
> Thou'rt risen, my bands are all untied,
> And now Thou livest in me;
> When purified, made white, and tried,
> Thy glory then for me.

3. Pergamum: 'I have a few things against you' (2:12–17)

Pergamum was quite a place! It was the 'Washington' of
Asia, the Romans having made it the capital of the province.
It had an enormous library containing some two hundred
thousand books and parchment was first made there. As
with the letter to Smyrna, this letter is contemporary with
a capital 'C', for both deal with the pressures upon Christians
living in a hostile world and in a society which largely has
abandoned God, His laws and His values.

The call to be watchful
'Be watchful!' sums up Christ's message here. He describes
Pergamum as 'where Satan has his throne' (13), which
reminds us that Satan is the author of evil, that he is always
active to blind unbelievers and to destroy the church, and
that from time to time (as here in Pergamum) he will make
a particular area of Christ's work the focus of his evil
attention and activity. Christ commends the Christians in
general terms for remaining true to His name and makes
special mention of Antipas, unknown to us but precious to
the Saviour. But then He has to say, 'I have a few things
against you' (14).

Satan has many devices and two of them are brought
into prominence here as a necessary focus for the believers'
watchfulness. *Satan persecutes* (13), and we know that he
is about this very business in many countries in the world
today. We have a massive obligation to pray for those of
our brethren in Christ who are on the receiving end of
Satan's persecuting attacks. But that is not all he does.

Satan seduces (14–16), and for us in the Western world
it is the subtleties of his seductions that we have special
need to be watchful about. In particular, he wishes to reduce
the distinctiveness and separation between the church and
the world, and in our own day he has had considerable
success. 'Why bother with religion?' is one of the questions
in people's minds, 'Or if you must, then why bother just
with Christianity?' Pergamum was infested with idolatry.
There was the cult of emperor worship ('Caesar is Lord'),
and the worship of Aesculapius, a 'god of healing' who was
worshipped under the emblem of a serpent. In addition to

this, the whole place was stacked out with altars, pride of place being given to one to Zeus. It is just the same in our present society — cults, sects, religions, mosques, multi-faith services in Anglican cathedrals and elsewhere, the teaching of comparative religion in schools and the general air of 'sink-your-differences-religion' and 'pot-pourri belief'. We need a fresh dose of Acts 4:12, with its insistence upon the uniqueness and exclusiveness of Christianity — the very truth the Lord Jesus Christ Himself insisted upon in John 14:6.

Or another line of seduction from Satan changes the question slightly: 'Why bother with a holy life?' He knows the power and effect of godliness, the massive potential of lives which adorn the gospel, and so he raises this question and whispers it seductively into our ears. Mention is made of those who followed the teaching of Balaam (14) and of the Nicolaitans (15). The reference to Balaam and Balak takes us back to Numbers 22—24, where they used idolatry and fornication as snares to trap the Israelites, and the putting of Balaam-Balak and the Nicolaitans side by side in Revelation 2 warns us against the danger of giving in to a life of freedom, licence and immorality. Satan presses this seduction very especially upon new Christians: 'Don't change too much! Why stick out? Why let people call you old-fashioned? Why not be the life and soul of the party? Everyone else is doing this, that or the other, so why aren't you?', though none are exempt from his assaults in this realm. We are not to listen to him. We are not to be taken in by him.

God's own Word, the sword of Christ's mouth (16; cf. 12; 1:16), is to be our rule and that Word insists that holiness, separateness and distinctiveness are to be every Christian's concern. 'But just as he who called you is holy, so be holy in all you do; for it is written, "Be holy, because I am holy"' (1 Peter 1:15—16). 'Holiness is not an optional extra in the Christian life; it is obligatory on every Christian to seek holiness. It is the end towards which every believer must discipline himself, and the goal towards which he must move every day.'[11] Christ is right; Satan is wrong. Christ is true; Satan is a liar. And so far as the church itself is concerned, Scripture teaches that whenever the children of God are obedient, separated and spiritual, then they are defended by God and their borders are increased. But when they neglect these weighty matters then everything goes wrong internally (cooling of devotion, sapping of spiritual energy, dulling of vision, soured relationships, eruption of strife) and their enemies outside invade them and defeat them. We have been warned!

More precious promises

Once again Christ gives a twofold promise (17) — the hidden manna and the white stone. To what is He referring?

What is 'the hidden manna' which the Lord Jesus Christ will give to the overcomers? God provided manna for His people's nourishment and support in the wilderness (Exodus 16). But have a look at what Jesus says in John 6:32–33. So the promise has to do with enjoying Christ, the One who nourishes us in the things of eternal life. And the manna is 'hidden' because the world knows nothing of it — those who belong to the world are strangers to the enjoyment of Christ's unchanging love, the enjoyment of meditating upon His glory, of enjoying Him in the assembly of the saints meeting for worship or meeting with Him on our own in the secret place. And all this enjoyment of Christ is but a foretaste of and preparation for enjoying Him in the glory of heaven itself. The best is always yet to come!

What is the 'white stone'? We cannot be certain, but this may derive from the tesserae (little stones of friendship) upon which was inscribed a combination of letters exclusive to some particular house. These stones were issued to various friends who then 'had free access to the house and a standing invitation to its hospitality. When a citizen of Pergamum became a Christian he immediately became a suspect of the state: this made him unwelcome to social functions and so his tessera was withdrawn.'[12] Our Lord Jesus Christ, however, will never withdraw any of His promises from us. 'Stone' stands for durability and imperishability; 'white' represents beauty, holiness and glory; and 'new name' speaks of the character and citizenship which belong uniquely to the servant of God. And if you put all of that together, this is what you get: the holiness without which none of us shall see the Lord! It is the gorgeous (and certain) prospect of the Christian free from the power, presence and frustration of sin, new through and through, conformed to Christ's own likeness. When all the world's bright lights are beginning to fade for the very last time, all those who belong to the Lord Jesus Christ will be coming into their heavenly and unfading inheritance!

4. Thyatira: 'You tolerate that woman Jezebel' (2:18–29)

On the letters go, this time to Thyatira, a town of great wealth, but lacking natural fortifications and so open to enemy attack. It was a city of trade guilds for people like wool-workers, linen-workers, dyers, tanners, potters, leather-workers and so on. It is fair to draw an analogy between these guilds and our trade unions in that they purported to 'protect' the workers and their jobs. But at the same time they were a real threat to the Christians. Why? Well, each guild had a 'guardian god'. If you wanted to get on in your job then you had to belong to the guild (a closed shop?); but if you belonged to the guild you had to worship its god, attend its guild festivals, eat food part of which was offered to this god and then take part in the X-certificate party afterwards. So inevitably there was great pressure put upon the Christians to conform to the world. What should they do? What would you do? The choice is a stark one: either leave the union, lose your job and make your family go without; or else stay in and deny your Lord! So there were problems for the church members in their life in the city, but all was not thoroughly well within the church either.

The good side
There was an attractive aspect to church life at Thyatira and the Lord Jesus Christ draws attention to it in verse 19. It seems best to take His comment 'I know your deeds' as the general statement which is then specified in four different aspects: 'your love and faith, your service and perseverance'. These are all bound up together. We might notice particularly their 'service'. The word means 'ministry', and the picture is of people giving themselves to and spending

themselves without reserve in gospel work and compassionate ministry inside and outside the household of faith —
such that if, for example, a brother or sister was taken ill,
the pastor would have to be a pretty alert man if he was to
get to visit them before anyone else, or if someone was in
particular need of help or assistance they would all very
naturally and spontaneously be rallying around with practical
help.

So once more, the Saviour does not let work done for Him
go unnoticed or unpraised.

The bad side
But verses 20—25 reveal a more serious problem — indeed
there was the problem itself and then the fact that the
church just put up with it rather than doing anything about
it. The problem was a woman in the congregation called
Jezebel — that was probably her real name, unless Jesus
called her that because she was reminiscent of the Old
Testament Jezebel (1 Kings 16—21). She called herself
(notice that!) a 'prophetess' — one who was empowered
with authority to declare God's Word and God's will to
the church, in direct contradiction, of course, to those
Scriptures (like 1 Timothy 2:11—15) which forbid women
to teach or have authority over men. That is why the church
is not free to have women preachers, elders or ministers;
those churches which do have them are in flagrant breach
of God's decrees for His church. If the question is raised,
'But what about Philip's "four unmarried daughters who
prophesied"?' (Acts 21:9), there is no indication that they
exercised any formal role or held any office or had any
following in the church — that would not have been. Indeed,
all the Acts reference tells us is the simple fact that in those
early church days, when the gift of prophecy was still in
operation, these four members of the church at Caesarea
had that gift. That in no way contradicts my remarks about
Jezebel or my application of 1 Timothy 2. Quite apart
from the fact that her teaching was evil, Jezebel was actually
a teacher and, amazingly, an accepted and acceptable one!

Anyway, this Jezebel was making plenty of noise in the
church at Thyatira and was claiming the inspiration of God
for what was evil and vile teaching, teaching which the Lord

Jesus Christ Himself dubs as 'Satan's so-called deep secrets' (24). From the description of her teaching given in verse 20 it seems that her line was 'The best way to conquer the world is to become familiar with its ways through personal experience, for that way you'll know what you're talking about and you'll have a firmer authority and wider sphere of influence.' Maybe too she urged the old error that 'The more you descend deliberately into the depths of a life of sin, the more you'll appreciate the glory of Christ's great deliverance.'

And, as if this was not bad enough, the whole business was compounded by the church's toleration of her and her teaching — they tolerated her, put up with her and by their silence and lack of rebuke and discipline they by implication agreed with her. How much the danger and folly of antinomianism stick out here! As if God's grace gives us a licence to sin, or that His laws can be set aside! As a result Christ warns of His judgement upon Jezebel, and on those who associate with her, 'unless they repent of her ways' (22). This is sombrely pressed home by Christ as the Searcher (18, 23).

Let us remember that only the Word of God (the sixty-six books of the Bible from Genesis to Revelation) gives us a sure and unshakeable foundation in the midst of error, false claims and supposed 'words from the Lord'. The simple rule is this: if what is taught or claimed as from God is in any way contrary to the Scriptures or in collision with any part of them, it must be rooted out and rejected.

What a relief it is, though, to learn that there were at least some in Thyatira who had not gone along with Jezebel's teaching and example! (24). The Head of the church urges them to hold firm in the Christian life, and says to them, 'I will not impose any other burden on you.' In other words, they must continue to take care not to commit any of the sins connected with Jezebel and her cronies and not to engage in anything to do with idols.

Still more precious promises
The final section of the letter (26–29) provides another of these twofold promises which remind us of the eternal dimensions of the Christian life. The promise this time to

overcomers, those who prove by their perseverance in the doing of the will of God that they are truly His, is of sharing Christ's rule (26—27) and sharing Christ's glory (28).

Our sharing of Christ's rule arises out of our union by faith with Him — verse 26b is true for the Christian because verse 27 is true for Christ. The Old Testament background is the quote from Psalm 2, which is a classic statement of the world's opposition to God and imaginings of its success. But, as that psalm declares, real authority and power rest not with the nations of the world but with the Lord Jesus Christ — that authority has been delivered to the Son by the Father (Matthew 28:18) and will be manifested supremely in the overpowering of the nations and their submission to Him at the end of the age. For while Christ's judgements are being meted out all the time (which we shall see clearly when we study the seals, trumpets and bowls), there is going to be a full and final work done by Christ against all His enemies — nations, systems, philosophies, false religions and individuals. And, in connection with all this, the humblest subject of the kingdom of God will have a part to play. We shall sit down with Christ on His judgement throne and join with Him in trying, condemning and consigning to judgement the enemies of Christ and His church. Is that not amazing?

Then there is our sharing of Christ's glory. If you compare this with 22:16 you will see that 'the morning star' is quite plainly a reference to Christ Himself. And a comparison with Daniel 12:3 and Matthew 13:43 shows that the brightness of the Saviour's glory and the shining of the righteous is what is in view. Sanctification's goal is not just a dream: 'When He appears, we shall be like Him, for we shall see Him as He is'! (1 John 3:2.)

4.
From Sardis to Laodicea

Please read Revelation 3

Christ's letters to the seven churches continue as we move
into the third chapter of the book.

5. Sardis: 'Wake up!' (3:1—6)

Sardis would have looked good on a holiday postcard. It
was a wealthy and prosperous city, standing in a command-
ing position on a hill. But there was more to Sardis than
met the eye!

The danger of false reputations
As before, the Lord Jesus Christ opens His account with
a description of Himself drawn from the vision in chapter 1.
And straight away He pinpoints the appalling problem from
which the church at Sardis was suffering. Indeed, a more
dire situation is hard to imagine. The church was dead!
Yet there is worse to come! The church did not realize it
and other churches who still looked up to her did not realize
it either. See what Christ says: 'You have a reputation of
being alive, but you are dead' (1). A dead church that
thought it was alive! As Dr Hendriksen has put it, 'Sardis
was a very "peaceful" church. It enjoyed peace, but it was
the peace of the cemetery!'

What a searching assessment for them to hear! How it
should stir us up — each one of us — that Christ would
never have cause to say it of the church to which we belong!
There is a clear connection between the condition of the
church at Sardis and the warning of Paul to Timothy of the

possibility of 'having a form of godliness but denying its power' (2 Timothy 3:5). It is not that there was nothing going on at Sardis, for Jesus says, '**I know your deeds**'; but He goes on to say in verse 2, '**I have not found your deeds complete in the sight of my God.**' Before God the church was the very opposite of what she was before men. There were deeds, there was activity — but there was the vital ingredient lacking: true spiritual life. There was form without power. There were lots of dead people hard at work!

The great thing to learn is this: there are certain things which can secure a church a good name and reputation for itself and which can make its own members imagine all is well. Yet, important and desirable things though these are, they are not of themselves alone a sure indication of healthy spiritual life. Among such matters we might list great numbers, attentiveness to worship with lusty singing and vigorous 'Amens', not a weeknight free of some sort of activity, ample money in the collection box, the absence of immoral conduct or party strife, plenty of religious conversation and a correct doctrinal basis. Upon the last two on our list, C. H. Spurgeon comments: 'There may be a savour of religion about a man's conversation, and yet it may be a borrowed flavour, like hot sauces used to disguise the staleness of ancient meat,' and 'It [the doctrinal basis] may have been departed from, or a church may put the creed in place of the Saviour, or its members may have gone soundly to sleep upon its sound creed.' A dead minister and a dead church! Remember that many a dying patient makes a brave show of life when he is just dropping into the grave.

So Christ's exhortation is a rousing one: '**Wake up! Strengthen what remains . . .**' (2). Remember — obey — repent! And if not, Christ will come like a thief, remove the lampstand from its place and, lo and behold, the church will have died in her sleep without being disturbed (3). The church would no longer be a church of Jesus Christ. He would have removed His Spirit, His Word, His light, His power, His presence — Himself. Ichabod — the glory will have departed.

The encouragement to the faithful

Happily there were still 'a few people in Sardis' of whom all the above was not true. So once again the Lord Jesus Christ has some lovely things to say to the overcomers. To encourage them to remain alive and awake (as well as to give a further incentive to the others to seek Christ afresh), He gives a most beautiful threefold promise which adds up to a glorious picture of the Christian's inheritance (4–5).

Walking with Christ 'dressed in white' looks forward to when we shall be with Christ, sanctified, victorious, 'a radiant church, without stain or wrinkle or any other blemish, but holy and blameless' (Ephesians 5:27). Never having your name erased from the book of life does not, of course, imply that it is possible for even a single one of those who, before the foundation of the world, were chosen by God in Christ for everlasting life and glory to perish; rather it reminds us that as the days go by in church life, there are those of whom it appears that their names have been written in the book of life, but their subsequent relapse into unbelief, sin and the world shows that 'They went out from us, but they did not really belong to us' (1 John 2:19). In contrast, those who are truly saved, those who have made their 'calling and election sure' (2 Peter 1:10) through a faithful and holy life and battle in the midst of a hostile world and sometimes even a hostile church, may rest secure. Toplady sums it up exquisitely:

> My name from the palms of His hands
> Eternity will not erase;
> Impressed on His heart it remains
> In marks of indelible grace;
> Yes, I to the end shall endure
> As sure as the earnest is given;
> More happy, but not more secure,
> The glorified spirits in heaven.

And having Jesus acknowledge your name before His Father and His angels — can you contemplate the joy of that? 'Come, you who are blessed by my Father, take your inheritance, the kingdom prepared for you since the creation of the world' (Matthew 25:34).

6. Philadelphia: 'I have placed before you an open door' (3:7—13)

Encouragement all the way is the keynote of Christ's message to the Christians at Philadelphia. The root of the name means 'brotherly love'. The town nestled in a valley on an important road some twenty-eight miles east of Sardis and had been founded with the intention of being the centre for the spread of Greek language and customs. The Christians there were a company of people who were walking with the Lord in the light of His Word, earnestly seeking to honour and glorify His name in their life together. So the Head of the church sets before them a threefold promise — the promise of an open door (7—9), the promise of being kept from the hour of trial (10—11), and the promise of absolute security (12—13).

The promise of an open door
The church had 'little strength' (8), which I take to mean that as the world counts strength in numbers and influence, then Philadelphia did not appear to be in the top league. But her spiritual condition was very different, again in the face of harsh opposition from 'the synagogue of Satan' (8—9). The actual promise Christ gives to them amounts to a firm assurance of great success in evangelism and gospel labour. It is worth comparing the similar picture in Acts 14:27; 1 Corinthians 16:9; 2 Corinthians 2:12 and Colossians 4:3 to confirm this interpretation. The gospel would be preached, heard and received!

This promise is wonderfully underscored by Christ's designation of Himself in verse 7 as the One 'who holds the key of David', as well as the rest of that same verse. The Old Testament background for the phrase 'key of David' is Isaiah 22:22. Isaiah pronounces there God's judgement upon Shebna, the king's treasurer and chief officer; the office will be taken away from him and given to Eliakim, the son of Hilkiah, a more worthy character. So this 'power of the key' gave authority to determine who should enter the king's presence and who should not. To the Lord Jesus Christ belongs the ultimate key of David, for He has said, 'No one comes to the Father except through me' (John

14:6). It is Christ Himself who adds to His church, He alone who opens up the way to God, He alone who saves. The hymn-writer Fanny J. Crosby puts it like this:

> To God be the glory! Great things He hath done!
> So loved He the world that He gave us His Son,
> Who yielded His life an atonement for sin
> And opened the life-gate that we may go in.
>
> Oh, perfect redemption, the purchase of blood!
> To every believer the promise of God;
> The vilest offender who truly believes,
> That moment from Jesus a pardon receives.

The promise of being kept from the hour of trial

The Bible is always absolutely true and absolutely realistic. Here the Philadelphian Christians are warned of '**the hour of trial that is going to come upon the whole world to test those who live on the earth**' (10). In the immediate context that refers to a wave of anti-Christian persecution and anti-gospel fury that was going to sweep through the entire then-known world, when the loyalty of those who confessed Christ as their Saviour and King would be tested to the limit. Yet there is a wider reference, for such waves have been regular features of the history of the church in the world — the Roman Catholic persecution of the evangelical martyrs at the time of the Reformation when many went to the scaffold and stake, the persecution against the Scottish Covenanters in the seventeenth century for insisting upon what they rightly regarded as the crown rights of Jesus Christ over His church and present-day persecution and imprisonment of Christians in the Soviet Union, Hungary, Romania and other places are some obvious examples. So Christ's warning here is both specific and general — another indication of the timelessness of this book we are studying.

But how are we to apply the promise of 'being kept'? Certainly not by a secret rapture of the church, for no such thing exists here or anywhere else in Christ's teaching. Rather is it a rich and glorious promise of the Lord's keeping of His church to the very end. The verb can be rendered 'keep you right through', so the meaning is Christ's work of assisting, enabling, protecting and preserving His people, even in the worst of times. Even those who have suffered (or will yet suffer) 'to the point of death' (2:10) are just as much 'kept' by Jesus as those whose 'lives' are not required.

We do not know what is coming, but we have this promise from the Saviour and the prospect of verse 11! Jesus says, '**I am coming soon.**' 'This to the struggling church and waiting believer is the sum of all promises. He comes in the prompt and mighty supports of His Spirit, in the deliverances of His Providences, in the reception of the disembodied spirit to Himself; but these are but the foretastes of the triumph at His second visible appearing. This is the assurance that soon the struggle will be ended, the battle fought, the victory won; that soon not only shall temptation cease to harrass, and indwelling sin to pollute, and hell to assault, and the purified spirit soar away to be with the spirits of just men made perfect; but that death itself, the last enemy, shall be destroyed, and the body itself raised and fashioned like unto Christ's glorious body, and the whole perfected church be admitted to the full glories of the resurrection state and the eternal kingdom.'[13]

The promise of absolute security

We shall leave any comment upon 'the new Jerusalem' until we come to it in chapter 21. Suffice it to say for the time being that Christ's promise of writing upon them '**the name of my God . . . the name of the city of my God . . . and . . . my new name**' all speak of our possession by God, our eternal belonging to him and our heavenly citizenship. Your name is an indication of who you are!

For now, let us concentrate upon the promise to overcomers: '**I will make [you] a pillar in the temple of my God**' (12). 'Temple' here stands not for a literal building but for God dwelling among His people, who know Him and are known by Him in close fellowship. But where does the pillar come in? It stands for that which abides and stands firm. The Philadelphia region was subject to earthquakes which caused pillars to topple, so that Christians would quickly grasp Christ's message. The Lord's people are not collapsing pillars but abiding pillars.

In summary, then, to be made a pillar in the temple of God is to enter for ever into the closest, richest, loveliest, sweetest, brightest, most blissful relationship imaginable with God in heaven.

> 'One thing I ask of the Lord,
>   this is what I seek:
> that I may dwell in the house of the Lord
>   all the days of my life,
> to gaze upon the beauty of the Lord
>   and to seek him in his temple'
>   (Psalm 27:4).

7. Laodicea: 'You are neither cold nor hot' (3:14–22)

This is one of the most amazing portions of Scripture, for this reason: Christ declares here that there is something that makes Him sick, something that nauseates Him. He is addressing the church at Laodicea in the last of these seven letters. Laodicea was an important city in Phrygia, very prosperous in its industry and commerce. The church is mentioned by Paul in Colossians 2:1. What does the Lord Jesus Christ do?

He analyses their problem

With absolute skill the divine Physician puts His finger right upon the sore spot. The Christians were lukewarm. They were not hot and they were not cold; just lukewarm. They were tepid, flabby, half-hearted, limp, ready to compromise rather than stand firm, listless, having lost all concern to grow and having given up any desire for vigorous spiritual activity, worship or gospel labour. Like a hot meal that has cooled down and begun to congeal, or a cold meal that has warmed up in the sun and begun to curl at the edges (how unappetizing!), these Laodicean Christians sickened the Lord Jesus Christ. He was so disgusted with their state, as they just sat there, that He said, 'I am about to spit you out of my mouth' (16). May we say this carefully and reverently: they made Christ want to throw up. That, quite frankly, is the effect our lukewarmness has upon Him.

To make matters worse, however, the Laodicean estimate of themselves was that they were rich, wealthy and not needing anything. Christ's assessment, though, was rather different. **'But you do not realize that you are wretched, pitiful, poor, blind and naked'** (17).

How far a church can fall! How can we read this and not tremble? Yet even in a condition as terrible as this, the Lord Jesus is tender and gracious. Why? **'Those whom I love I rebuke and discipline'** (19). His church is His church. He gave Himself up for her. He shed His blood for her.

> From heaven He came and sought her
> To be His holy bride,
> With His own blood He bought her,
> And for her life He died.
> (Samuel J. Stone).

He advocates a prescription

'I counsel you to buy from me,' He begins in verse 18. Christ is not content just to let us be, if an individual Christian backslides or a church becomes a shame. So having exposed all that is wrong, He is now at pains to put things right. And He does so in a most startling manner. Let me explain.

The city of Laodicea was a great centre for three things: finance and banking, clothing manufacture (famous for its black wool), and medicine (with an eye salve called collysion which reputedly worked wonders). The Lord Jesus Christ uses each of these features to press His spiritual counsel home upon their consciences. What He says in verse 18 could be paraphrased like this: 'You are convinced of your wealth, but you are spiritually bankrupt and need not actual gold but the gold of God's currency – fresh supplies of God's grace to forgive you, God's wisdom to direct you, God's strength to support you and God's joy to abide in your souls. You are convinced of your great clothing trade, but you are spiritually naked and need the white raiment and covering that come from the sanctifying work of the Holy Spirit in you and upon you, creating spiritual beauty and bringing forth spiritual fruit. You are convinced of your marvellous eye-potion, but you are spiritually blind and can no longer discern how things really are with you. You no longer look up to God and see His face, or have eyes to weep for sinners, or look into His Word. You no longer have any vision of the work I have given you to do or the glory that is to be revealed.' In each case, Christ urges them to apply to Him, for of Him the apostle Paul speaks when he says, 'My God will meet all your needs according to his glorious riches in Christ Jesus' (Philippians 4:19).

The verb 'buy' does not imply human ability. It is that buying of which the prophet Isaiah speaks when God calls His people to buy 'without money and without cost' (Isaiah 55:1). For salvation in the first place and then all the continuing blessings of the Christian life are all of grace.

He asserts a priority

We come now to that very famous Bible verse, Revelation 3:20! Without any hesitation it would receive my nomination for the award of 'the most regularly misinterpreted verse of Scripture'. We have seen already that Christ is addressing His church — it may, in its lukewarm condition, be 'only just' His church, but it is still His church. So He is addressing believers, though I grant that, as in many churches, some unbelievers may have crept in on the grounds that they seemed genuine so far as the elders could discover at the time.

The point, then, at which so many have gone wrong is to treat this verse as first and foremost an evangelistic text — a situation which has not been helped one bit by Holman Hunt's painting 'The Light of the World', supposedly derived from this verse, with its picture of a forlorn-looking and impotent Christ knocking at the door which is meant to represent the sinner's heart, with the door handle very firmly on the inside! No! What this verse does picture is the glorious, risen, ascended all-powerful Lord Jesus Christ standing at the door of the church at Laodicea. As He stands there and knocks, He speaks to every individual in the church. They have 'put Him outside', we might say, with their neglect and arrogance, and He now appeals to them that they might be shaken out of their lukewarmness and their self-confidence and restored to new heights and depths of fellowship and communion with Him. In other words,

communion with Christ rather than union with Christ is
the theme! He knows that the best remedy for backsliding
is for the believer to be more fully and freshly taken up
with Him. That is why He speaks as He does.

Concerning our fellowship and communion with Christ,
there are several things here to notice. It is *real*: how much
do you know of it? It is *spiritual*, based upon spiritual
blessings and issuing in spiritual duties. It is *rich* — the
word for 'eat' (AV, 'sup') is not the language of 'I'll just
have a quick snack and be on my way,' or 'I won't take
my coat off, I'm not stopping.' The idea is of the supper
in Eastern lands, which was the best meal of the day, a
leisurely and lingering affair. In these days of rushed
activity, slot-machine quiet times, complaints about the
length of sermons and so on, how much time do you give
to communion with your Saviour? It is *mutual*, for Christ
says, 'I will come in and eat with him, and he with me'.
The Bible has a lot to say about the believer's desires for
fellowship with Christ, but it has no less to say about Christ's
own desire for fellowship with His people (cf. Song of
Solomon 2:14; 4:9–15; 8:13). It is *heavenly*. Listen to
John Flavel: 'Strive to come up to the highest attainment
of communion with God in this world, and be not contented
with just so much grace as will secure you from hell —
labour after such a height of grace and communion with
God as may bring you into the suburbs of heaven on
earth.'[14] The promise of verse 21 has heaven in view! And,
finally, it is *personal*. Christ says, 'if anyone . . .' The local
church to which you belong will only be a glory to God if
each individual (you and me) is right with God, walking
close to Him and having fellowship with Him. We cannot
hide behind each other.

He adds a promise

How delightful and encouraging these promises at the end
of each of the letters have been! And this final one is no
exception (21). This time the promise to the overcomers
is the assurance of sitting with Christ upon His throne.
And since Christ's throne is the Father's throne, what royal
glory awaits us!

So there are Christ's messages to the seven churches of

Asia — and to us. One church was loveless, one persecuted, one compromising, one over-tolerant, one dying, one with great opportunities opening up before it and one lukewarm. Here is the church of Christ on earth in a wide variety of its aspects and conditions. We have dwelt closely upon these chapters 2 and 3 because they are so foundational to the whole book. Our need now is for urgent and serious self-examination and self-enquiry, as Christ, the glorious Head of His church, searches our hearts.

'He who has an ear, let him hear what the Spirit says to the churches.'

5.
Worship the Lord in the beauty of holiness

Please read Revelation 4

'A door was standing open in heaven'. Can you imagine the sight? Now that the messages to the seven churches have been made known safely to the apostle John, a new vista takes his attention. The same voice that he had heard speaking to him previously, which belonged to the Lord Jesus Christ, spoke to him again and invited him to take a glimpse inside heaven. Christ said to him, 'Come up here, and I will show you what must take place after this' (1).

Two things of importance need to be said straight away. First, notice the divine 'must'. The old comment that history is 'His story' is worth recalling. Matthew Henry has remarked somewhere that 'Whatever is transacted on earth is first designed and settled in heaven.' The other thing is this: chapters 4 and 5 are not only an entity in themselves, but also stand at the head of the whole section comprising the opening of the seven seals, the blowing of the seven trumpets and the pouring out of the seven bowls. And what you have in this massive chunk of the book is not a chronology of history (one event following another in chronological order with identifiable events) but principles of history (a picture of the things that are happening and the conditions that are obtaining again and again in the world, not least throughout the period from the resurrection and ascension of the Lord Jesus Christ until the coming of the glorious day which God has fixed for His return).

Once again John was 'in the Spirit' (2). The repetition of this phrase which we met earlier, in 1:10, suggests, maybe, that between the dictating of the seven letters and this vision of heaven John had returned for a short season to his regular state of mind. To the explanations of the phrase itself which we gave before, we may add this note from Ramsey: 'It was not a bodily, but a spiritual ascent. His whole consciousness was severed from all connection with this world and its sensible objects, and elevated into a higher state, where it was entirely controlled by the Spirit, alive only to sights and sounds presented by the Holy Spirit.' Ramsey also follows on with another remark which it would be profitable to record: 'These sights and sounds were not real, literal existences; it was not the real, actual heaven, the locality where the glorified Redeemer dwells with the spirits of His redeemed, which the apostle saw now in vision; but, as the imagination pictures before itself creations of its own as vividly as though beheld by the outward eye, so the Spirit of God now made these pictures of spiritual and future things to pass before the mental vision of the apostle.'[15]

The vision of heaven in chapters 4 and 5 is a unity, with two clear parts. In chapter 4, the focus is upon God in His sovereignty, majesty and holiness, while in chapter 5 the spotlight falls upon the Lord Jesus Christ in His redeeming love and glory. The section abounds in rich spiritual instruction, not least upon the subject of worship.

1. The sight John saw

How do you describe what God looks like? What John saw here was really a vision of God, but he does not actually call it that. We can list the many attributes of God and declare many things concerning His ways, but we are faced with this problem: God cannot in Himself ultimately be described. He is beyond our telling.

The first thing that took John's attention was *the throne and its occupant*: 'There before me was a throne in heaven with someone sitting on it' (2) — God upon the throne. But 'To whom will you compare me? Or who is my equal? says the Holy One' (Isaiah 40:25). The way that it is given to John to set about describing God here is to do so in the language of precious stones. He has to say that 'The one who sat there had the appearance of . . .' Had the appearance of what? Look at verse 3.

'Jasper': this is a transparent stone, rather like a diamond, yet which offers to the eye a variety of most vivid colours as it is viewed from different angles and in different lights. It signified to John, and it signifies to us, the glorious and infinite perfection of God, and especially the purity and dazzling brightness of His holiness.

'Carnelian': also called the sardine stone, this is blood red, and without hesitation speaks to us of the inflexibility and uncompromising character of God's justice and the fierceness of His wrath.

'Rainbow': described here not in its usual multi-coloured aspect (red, orange, yellow, green, blue, indigo, violet) but 'resembling an emerald'. There is never any doubt concerning the rainbow. Ever since the days of God's covenant with Noah (Genesis 9) it has spoken of covenant mercy, grace and love. If you ask why it should resemble an emerald (which is green), then maybe the restfulness and peace granted to the believer as a result of God's mercy are chiefly in view. Green is the most restful of colours, hence God's choice of it for the trees and fields and so much more of His creation. My own favourite colour is red, but can you imagine how it would be for our eyes if all those things which God has painted green were bright red instead? How blessed are the words of the apostle in Romans 5:1–2: 'Since we have been justified through faith, we have peace with God through our Lord Jesus Christ, through whom we have gained access by faith into this grace in which we now stand.'

These three precious stones (jasper, carnelian, emerald) taken together add up to what is in effect a summary of the gospel: God's holiness, His hatred of sin and the condemnation that the sinner is under as a result, but then His grace, mercy and love seen in Jesus — that love which passes praises, passes knowledge and passes telling, that love 'so full, so rich, so free, that brings a rebel sinner such as me nigh unto God'!

The noises proceeding from the throne and the reference to the Holy Spirit (5), together with 'what looked like a sea of glass, clear as crystal' which was 'before the throne' (6) add to the overall picture of the awe-inspiring magnificence of God. We do not have to find a separate

interpretation for every single detail — that is where many
students of this book have gone wrong.

But John saw something else as well: '**Surrounding the
throne were twenty-four other thrones, and seated on them
were twenty-four elders**' (4). His eye had transferred from
the dominant throne with its glorious Occupant to *the other
thrones, each with its own occupant*, which surrounded it.
Who are these elders? We are familiar with the term in the
New Testament as the designation of those officers in the
church of Christ whose call to preach, teach, pastor and
rule has been received from the Head of the church and
recognized by His body in a given locality. They are the
angels of the churches whom we met in the preceding chapters. But the word is not used in that sense here. The clue
to the right interpretation is their number — John saw
twenty-four of them. Simple mathematics reminds us that
24 is made up of 12 + 12, and Bible knowledge teaches us
that there were twelve tribes of Israel in the Old Testament
and twelve apostles in the New Testament. So these twenty-
four elders stand symbolically as representatives of the
whole church of God throughout the old and the new dispensations. They stand for the entire church of God, having been
redeemed by the blood of Christ, having overcome in the
battle, having 'fought the good fight . . . finished the race . . .
kept the faith' (2 Timothy 4:7), and now sharing with
Christ in the promised royal dominion and glory. All those
wonderful promises appended to the letters to the seven
churches will come true! '**Dressed in white**' shows that we
shall be thoroughly sanctified at last, and the crowns of gold
confirm that we shall be victorious at last. Everything will
have been worth it! William Cowper wrote:

> Dear dying Lamb! Thy precious blood
> Shall never lose its power,
> Till all the ransomed church of God
> Be saved, to sin no more.

There you have it!

2. The song John heard

There is plenty of singing going on in the book of Revelation!
On this occasion it came first of all from some very strangely
described characters: 'four living creatures . . . covered with
eyes, in front and behind' (6). Look at the details recorded
in verses 6—8. We might well say of them that they must
have been no beauties! Who were they?

Some say, the powers of creation; some say, the ministers
of the gospel; some say, the cherubim: and some identify
them with the four Gospel portraits of the Lord Jesus Christ
(the lion — Christ as King of the Jews in Matthew: the ox —
Jesus the obedient Servant in Mark; the man — Jesus in His
humanity in Luke; the eagle — Jesus Christ as the eternal
Son in John). Of these varied suggestions, perhaps the
cherubim fits best, not least bearing in mind the similarities
between this passage and chapters 1—10 of the prophecy
of Ezekiel (cf. Ezekiel 10:20). The cherubim are the highest
order of angels and their special task is to guard the holy
things of God (cf. Genesis 3:24; Exodus 25:20). Of them,
Dr Hendriksen remarks that they are 'in strength like the
lion, in ability to render service like the ox, in intelligence
like man . . . and in swiftness like the eagle'. They appear
in this present vision, no doubt, in order to enhance further
the significance and glory of the throne of God.

More important, though, is what they are doing. And the
answer to that is that they are engaging day and night in
songs of worship and praise to God, setting forth His glory.
Their own song is recorded in verse 8, and the song in which
the elders joined is found in verse 11. In each case God
Himself is the focus and object of their adoration. They are
taken up with Him, in particular with His holiness, His
everlastingness and His sovereign power in creation.

It is worth stopping for a moment to gather up some
vital applications concerning the worship of God. First of
all, we learn from this chapter that *God alone* (the triune
God — Father, Son and Holy Spirit) *is the object of our
worship*. Not the creature, not the Virgin Mary, not anyone or anything . . . but God! God Himself and God alone!
'**You are worthy, our Lord and God, to receive glory and
honour and power**' (11). Worship is 'worthship' — the

declaring of the worthiness of God. What you think of God will be reflected in how you worship Him – in the worth you ascribe to Him. And the character and attributes of God call forth worship.

God is holy

The prophet Habakkuk declares of God: 'Your eyes are too pure to look on evil' (Habakkuk 1:13), and the apostle John declares that 'God is light; in him there is no darkness at all' (1 John 1:5). When the Bible speaks of God's holiness it means His separateness from and exaltation above all His creation, His absolute perfection and excellence (in Himself, His Word, His works and His ways), and the complete absence of any sinfulness or impurity in Him. Truly He is 'majestic in holiness' (Exodus 15:11). Jonathan Edwards has written in one place, 'Holiness is more than a mere attribute of God – it is the sum of all His attributes, the outshining of all that God is.' The Bible is full of this.

And it is because God is holy that He cannot leave sin to go unpunished. It is because He is holy that none of our own miserable efforts can haul ourselves up to God or recommend ourselves to Him. And it is because God is holy that He has provided for us in His Son, Jesus Christ, a Mediator who has satisfied God's searching holiness and unswerving justice and opened up for us 'a way back to God from the dark paths of sin'. Is it any wonder that the four living creatures, as with those other creatures (the seraphim of Isaiah 6) before them, expressed God's holiness as thrice-holiness? **'Holy, holy, holy is the Lord God Almighty'** (8).

God is everlasting

He is **'the Lord God Almighty, who was, and is, and is to come'** (8). 'The three tenses of the Lord God Almighty's existence express eternity,' writes William Still. This too should call forth vigorous praise and adoration from the believer. Our God is past finding out. We cannot contain Him or pocket Him up. The very contemplation of everlastingness blows our finite minds.

God is the Creator
'You created all things, and by your will they were created
and have their being' (11). Calvin has remarked that creation
is 'the theatre of His glory', and in saying that he is only
echoing what the psalmist David uttered in a psalm like
Psalm 19. Evolution is one of the devil's most successful
con-tricks and needs to be exposed as such. Spurgeon·has
called it an 'abyss of absurdity'.

The truth of the matter is that God has created all things.
'The earth is the Lord's, and everything in it, the world,
and all who live in it' (Psalm 24:1). 'The heavens declare
the glory of God; the skies proclaim the work of his hands'
(Psalm 19:1). 'For he spoke, and it came to be; he commanded, and it stood firm' (Psalm 33:9). And the climax
of God's creating work was man himself — made sovereignly
and especially by God in his own image and likeness (Genesis
1:26—27). We have been created by God, made to know
God and fitted to praise, worship and adore Him. 'Glorify
the Lord with me; let us exalt his name together' (Psalm
34:3).

Do you live to worship God? Do you delight to ascribe
to Him the glory and honour which are due to Him? How
do you view the hymns you sing in church and in the prayer
meeting — are they truly vehicles of praise to God, as you
pour out your heart and soul in worship before Him? Is
God exalted in your midst? Or is He dragged down to your
own level and treated as your best pal in a carnal, gimmicky
manner that is an abomination to Him?

And remember this: God deserves and is worthy not
only of the praise of our lips, but the praise of our whole
lives. The twenty-four elders got down off their thrones
and fell down before God, laying their crowns before Him.
What a picture of whole-hearted consecration, dedication
and obedience!

> O worship the Lord in the beauty of holiness,
> Bow down before Him, His glory proclaim;
> With gold of obedience, and incense of lowliness,
> Kneel and adore Him, the Lord is His name
>   (J. S. B. Monsell).

There is to be nothing 'Sunday only' about our worship of God. Is your daily spiritual discipline in the Word and prayer a praise to God, as you humbly and longingly seek His presence? Is your hour-by-hour mortifying of sin in your members a praise to Him, or through your carelessness about growth in grace and holiness do you grieve the Father who set His love upon you, the Son who shed His blood for you and the Holy Spirit who has made you His temple? Is your marriage a praise to Him — husbands loving your wives and wives submitting to your husbands? What of your family life — parents training up your children in the way of the Lord and children obeying your parents in the Lord? Do you glorify God in the cheerful, diligent and honest manner in which you go about your daily work? Is God glorified in what you watch on television, in your choice of reading material and in the friendships you make? Is your bringing of a full tithe and other offerings done in a spirit of thankfulness and praise to the God who has given you everything you possess? Our God is a demanding God because He is who He is! Well may we sing, with Frances Ridley Havergal:

> Take myself, and I will be
> Ever, only, all for Thee.

The second thing we learn is this: while our praise will have as its great and constant theme God's grace towards us in salvation, another great subject for worship, as well as a great source of comfort for the Christian, is God's sovereignty (11). 'He's got the whole world in His hands' is not just a song to sing for the sake of it; it testifies to a great and firm truth which stays our souls. God sits upon the throne. What — on the throne of this world, with its political uncertainty, economic collapse, wars, terrorism, murder and disregard for the sanctity of life? On the throne of my life, with all my difficulties and perplexities, my struggles with indwelling sin, and my failures in service? Yes! Yes!

God is still on the throne
  And He will remember His own!
Though trials upset you and burdens distress you,
  He never will leave you alone.
God is still on the throne,
  And He will remember His own;
His promise is true — He will not forget you!
God is still on the throne.

But if you are not a Christian but should be reading this book, see who it is with whom you need to be reconciled, for you are His enemy! The living God, the God of history, the God of the universe is not some figment of a crazy Christian's imagination. You will have to stand before Him and give an account of every deed you have ever done, every word you have ever spoken and every thought you have ever entertained — whether you even acknowledge His existence and power right now or not!

6.
Worthy is the Lamb who was slain

Please read Revelation 5

We have already remarked that chapters 4 and 5 stand at the head of the rest of the book of Revelation and provide the backcloth against which we must interpret all the visions that follow. It is important to understand that chapter 5 is a continuation of the same vision John received in chapter 4, though the central focus changes and falls upon the second Person of the Trinity, the Lord Jesus Christ. We shall divide the material under the same two headings as before.

1. The sight John saw

There are five features in the vision that occupied John's attention one after the other. First, there was a *scroll* (1). It was held in God's right hand, completely covered with writing on both sides and sealed up with seven seals. What are we to make of that?

The scroll represents God's plan of history from eternity to eternity, a plan in which, of course, His church has a special part. History is not just a haphazard connection of chance happenings or encounters. 'Known unto God are all his works from the beginning of the world' (Acts 15:18, AV). He has great plans and purposes. Have a look, for example, at Isaiah 46:10. The whole course of future events and the whole arrangements of the ages to come are determined by God. He has left nothing out of His plans that should be there and His purposes are incapable of any failure in execution or any improvement. They are perfect as He is

perfect. No unforeseen contingencies can arise and nothing
is left unprovided for. That is why there is writing on both
sides, which is unusual for a scroll. It indicates completeness.

But why is the scroll sealed up? Because God's plan
is not only fixed, but secret — hidden from our eyes, unless
and until He should reveal it to us. Remember that the very
name of the book 'Revelation' means 'unveiling'. And why
seven seals? We shall have cause on several occasions to
remark upon the use and importance of numbers in
Revelation. Seven stands for perfection and fulness, as we
have already seen in the references to the Holy Spirit as
'the seven spirits of God' and the fact of the letters being
addressed to seven churches.

Then John saw *a mighty angel* (2) asking a question
of great moment in a loud voice: '**Who is worthy to break
the seals and open the scroll?**' The reason that is such an
important question is that unless someone is found to break
the seals and open the scroll, none of us will ever be any
the wiser regarding God's plans and purposes. We shall
know that He has them (verse 1 has shown us that), but
we shall neither know what the scroll contains nor, indeed,
will the events be carried out or accomplished.

What does John see next? Precisely this: *nothing happening* (3)! The mighty angel had bellowed so loudly that the
entire universe could hear. But nothing stirred and no one
answered. Behold the absolute impotence of any created
being or group of created beings to govern the world or
bring to pass God's everlasting kingdom! The challenge
has been put. We might say that the gauntlet has been thrown
down. Here is the big chance for those who think they
are someone to prove themselves. But no one in heaven
can help (not even the angels who are always before the
throne of God); no one on earth has power to do anything
(no man, no politician, prime minister or president, no
world banker or industrialist, no philosopher or leading
thinker, no pope or archbishop, no revolutionary hero);
and no one under the earth (no fallen angels, no spirits
of the departed, and not even the prince of darkness himself). This is a verse that puts creation firmly in its place.
The effect of this upon the apostle John was that he wept
and wept (4).

The fourth feature in the vision upon which John's gaze fell was *one of the elders* (5). We met the elders in the previous chapter, and one of their number came forward with good news: there is One, after all, who 'is able to open the scroll and its seven seals'. But who is it? Who can it be? It is the Lord Jesus Christ!

He is described here under two magnificent titles: 'the Lion of the tribe of Judah, the Root of David'. The first of these titles takes us back to Genesis 49:9—10, when the patriarch Jacob was giving his farewell words to his sons, in this case Judah. The lion invariably stands as a symbol of strength. It is the king of the beasts of the field, and so a fit symbol of conquering power. And just such power belongs to the Lord Jesus Christ. He has conquered Satan and triumphed over sin and death. The second of these titles (cf. Isaiah 11:1) reminds us that Christ is the One who has come, as promised, from the family line of David. He is the promised Messiah, God's own Son. He is the royal King, to whom is given all power and authority in heaven and earth. So He alone is in a position to open the scroll. He alone is worthy. He alone can declare God to man, for He alone in the unity of the Trinity is party and privy to all that the scroll contains.

So the last thing that took John's attention was *the Lord Jesus Christ Himself* (6—7). Yet there is something unexpected here. John saw not a lion but 'a Lamb, looking as if it had been slain, standing in the centre of the throne'. He who is the great strong lion is also the Lamb of God who was led to the slaughter for sinners. He has conquered, but not through force of arms or argument, not by warring or tearing His enemies apart, but by being slain. As we shall see from verse 9, He has conquered by His blood. The strange visionary details in verse 7 of the seven horns and the seven eyes speak of the all-powerfulness and all-knowingness of the Lord Jesus Christ, who is 'the power of God and the wisdom of God' (1 Corinthians 1:24), and who, after His death and resurrection, ascended again to heaven's glory and from there sent out His Holy Spirit.

This sight that so engrossed John should, now that we have begun to untangle it, give abundant comfort to you if you belong to Jesus. To you, as to John, are the words of the elder addressed: 'Do not weep!' Christ has conquered, and you are more than conquerors through Him! Do not despair, do not give up, do not weep, even though your corruptions are strong, your enemies are mighty and you may seem to be making little progress in the Christian life. The question is not of your own strength but of the powerful blood and perfect righteousness of your Lord Jesus!

Do not weep in the face of your great trials and troubles, your heartaches and afflictions. Every one of them is written in that scroll in the right hand of the One seated upon the throne, as part of the process needed for your refining. The Lord would sanctify to you your deepest distress, to use the hymn-writer's lovely phrase. If you have committed your poor helpless soul to the Saviour, then remember that everything about your case and condition is safe in His hands, for the Lamb who saved you is the Lion who protects you. The same hands that were nailed to the cross for your sins unfold your life's history day by day, and they do it with unerring wisdom and unfailing love so as to secure all the results God has promised you and purposed for you. And do not weep in the face of the sad and sorry state of the church with its heresies, divisions and the many attacks upon it. Mourn over it, to be sure, but do not despair, for we shall see one day just how futile is the opposition of earth and hell to the church of Christ. Has He not said, 'I will build my church, and the gates of hell will not overcome it'? (Matthew 16:18.)[16]

2. The song John heard

A glance through the remainder of chapter 5 will reveal that there followed three songs which fitted together perfectly: the song of the living creatures and the elders (8-10); the song of 'many angels, numbering thousands upon thousands, and ten thousand times ten thousand' (11-12); and finally all creation singing together (13). Then comes the climax of verse 14 — the cry of 'Amen' and the act of falling down and worshipping.

We are presented here with a picture of the worship which rightly belongs to the Lord Jesus Christ, to Him who is the delight of the Father, the delight of heaven, as well as the delight of believers upon the earth. The 'you are worthy' from 4:11 occurs again in 5:9, and the worthiness of Christ as the One to whom is due 'honour and glory and praise' is underscored in verse 12. Let us approach this section by means of the question: 'In what character is the Lord Jesus Christ worshipped and adored?'

First, as *the Mediator.* Only He was found worthy to take the scroll and break open its seals. And immediately upon this discovery heaven breaks out into praise. Only the Lord Jesus Christ could unfold the mysteries of God's will, for He is the key to all God's purposes. He is 'the Alpha and Omega' (cf. 1:8). He is the only One who reveals God to man and brings man to God. He Himself says, 'All things have been committed to me by my Father. No one knows the Son except the Father, and no one knows the Father except the Son and those to whom the Son chooses to reveal him' (Matthew 11:27). The apostle Paul declares, 'For there is one God and one mediator between God and men, the man Christ Jesus, who gave his life as a ransom for all men' (1 Timothy 2:5–6). And the apostle Peter insists that 'Christ died for sins once for all, the righteous for the unrighteous, to bring you to God' (1 Peter 3:18). There is a glorious unity of testimony upon Christ's work as Mediator throughout the whole of Scripture.

The great doctrine is plainly stated even way back in Genesis 28:12, for the Lord Jesus Christ is the 'stairway resting on the earth, with its top reaching to heaven' which runaway Jacob saw in his dream. This is the truth that the living creatures and the elders are singing about at the beginning of verse 9, arising from the humbling and thrilling realization that everything depends upon Christ's mediatorial work. Without it, we should have no knowledge of God, no salvation and no hope. You can never prize Christ too highly! C. H. Spurgeon, preaching upon this passage, remarks, 'No one else can go in for us to the august presence of the Most High, and take the title-deeds of grace into His hand on our behalf; but Christ can do it, and taking it He can unfold it and expound to us the wondrous purpose of electing love towards the chosen ones.'[17]

Secondly, as *our Redeemer.* He has 'purchased men for

God' (AV has 'redeemed us to God'). The essence of redemption is the buying back of something lost or gone astray by the payment of a price or ransom. We who were lost and guilty sinners have been purchased for God with the blood of Jesus. For He has not just revealed God's plans for the salvation of sinners; He has actually come into the world to save sinners. He has not merely proclaimed God's offer of salvation; He has provided salvation through Himself being slain. He is Himself 'the way and the truth and the life' (John 14:6). Words like 'slain', 'blood' and 'sacrifice' make us think of the whole business of Old Testament sacrifices. All those sacrifices pointed forward to the Lord Jesus Christ who 'offered for all time one sacrifice for sins' (Hebrews 10:12) — a sacrifice at once perfect, unrepeatable, incapable of improvement, thoroughly effective for dealing with sin and absolutely acceptable to God and approved by Him. And this is the glorious result — the redemption of the elect — **'men for God from every tribe and language and people and nation'** (cf. 7:9).

Thirdly, as *the Bestower of high dignities*. Verse 10 has links with 1:6, which I commented upon at the time. Have another look at what was said there. Here, as there, the emphasis is upon the high dignities and honours that are granted to every believer because of the Lord Jesus Christ — we are made a kingdom and are priests to serve God. In a phrase, you could say we live to God.

Fourthly, as *God*. We have stressed how chapters 4 and 5 are all one vision, so notice now how 4:11 ties up exactly with 5:12, not word for word as such but the point is this: the same ascription is given to both the Father and the Son. This is in line with Jesus' own words in John 5:23, 'that all may honour the Son just as they honour the Father. He who does not honour the Son does not honour the Father, who sent him.' In other words, Jesus is God! There can be no question or doubt about it and we need to proclaim the Godhead of the Lord Jesus Christ far and wide, not least to those both inside and outside the 'church' who deny it or dispute it.

The sevenfold doxology of verse 12 with the fourfold doxology of verse 13, **'to him who sits on the throne and to the Lamb'**, are an expression of the highest adoration that language can supply. Josiah Conder put it this way:

In Thee most perfectly expressed
The Father's glories shine;
Of the full Deity possessed,
Eternally divine:

Worthy, O Lamb of God, art Thou
That every knee to Thee should bow.

What response is it possible to make to all this? The
one word of the four living creatures is best — **'Amen'** (14).
Not a faint little murmur that can scarcely be heard, but a
sound like claps of thunder, an expression of confident
faith and glad worship, a thorough assent to all that has
been said — a cry of 'This is so! This is gloriously true!'
'And the elders fell down and worshipped.'

7.
Here is the news!

Here are the main news headlines for 1984, 1985, 1986 or any other year you care to name.

There will continue to be reports from different parts of the world of invasions, *coups d'état*, wars, fighting and terrorism. Inflation will continue to bite. Broadly speaking, the rich will remain rich and the poor will remain poor. Certain areas of the world will be struck by famine. Death will continue to rear its ugly head — every moment of every day some people will die. Christians will continue to be persecuted. But the glorious gospel of the Lord Jesus Christ will continue to ride on victoriously and many sinners will be saved!

All that is not idle speculation. I am merely taking Revelation 6:1—11 seriously! As we left chapter 5, the Lord Jesus Christ had taken the scroll 'from the right hand of him who sat on the throne'. That scroll, we said, was God's purposes in history, centred upon Christ, and all leading ultimately to the firm establishment of His glorious kingdom. It was sealed with seven seals. Now what we have right through from 6:1 to 8:1 is that one by one those seals are opened, and we see some of the things which have occurred in every age of history and are happening quite observably in the world around us — things which are necessary preludes to the return of the Lord Jesus Christ and the bringing of 'a new heaven and a new earth, the home of righteousness' (2 Peter 3:13). Again the timelessness of Revelation is seen. All of history is constantly under review, rather than the seals following some chronological sequence.

We shall look in this section at the first five seals, but shall start with the second. You'll see why!

The opening of the second seal: the rider on the fiery red horse

Read verses 3—4 through again. With each of the first four seals there is a horse and a rider, though with each seal something different is represented. The horse, again and again in Scripture, is a symbol of strength and an animal of war and battle. There is a remarkable picture of this in Job 39:19—25, which it would be good to stop and read right now.

The colour of the horse in the second seal is fiery red — the colour of wrath and anger, violence and bloodshed, lust and war. And we are told that the rider, with a large sword that is given to him, takes peace from the earth and makes men slay each other.

What we have represented here is clearly war and destruction, conflicts and divisions, hatreds and discords — all stemming from sin and the world's rejection of the gospel of peace with God. Sometimes people talk of universal peace, an abandonment of nuclear arms and maybe even an abandonment of arms altogether. Now it may be preferable — I'm sure it is — that we should not have nuclear arms in the world, but it is living in a dream to imagine that you can just do away with arms and suddenly (or ever) have universal peace in a sinful world. One aspect of sin is seen directly in war: lust for power and independence and greed for territory.

This rider on the fiery red horse will continue to make his presence felt this year and every year until Christ has returned. We shall hear constantly of 'wars and rumours of wars . . . such things must happen . . . nation will rise against nation and kingdom against kingdom' (Mark 13:7—8).

Yet all is not gloom, for it is the Lord Jesus Christ who opens this seal, it is He who holds the reins of history. Everything (yes, everything) will be made to fulfil His purposes and will contribute to bringing in His kingdom.

The opening of the third seal: the rider on the black horse

Read verses 5—6 through again. Black is the appropriate

colour this time, for we have a picture of the distress caused by famine and scarcity, a picture of economic troubles and biting inflation, where it costs a day's wages to buy a ration of wheat or three rations of barley. In other words, food is available, but at the price of your wages! The necessities of life take all you've got. But '**Do not damage the oil and the wine!**' Oil and wine here are symbols of luxury, indulgence and merriment. Some who are rich will continue so, enjoying their gourmet feasts and indulging themselves, while others starve and do not even have a day's ration of food. There will be butter mountains and wine lakes. It is all frighteningly contemporary.

Even inflation, however, serves the purposes of the Lord Jesus Christ — as a chastisement upon a rebellious earth and as a means to cause people to abandon their trust in riches or earthly and external things and to turn to Him who alone can give the bread of life and eternal riches that will never fade away. The message of Jesus on one occasion to a crowd of Jews who had gone after Him was this: 'Do not work for food that spoils, but for food that endures to eternal life, which the Son of Man will give you' (John 6:27).

The opening of the fourth seal: the rider on the pale horse

Read verses 7—8 through again. We use phrases like 'pale as death', 'white as a sheet', or 'he looks like death warmed up', all of which suit well the present context. When the Lord Jesus Christ opens the fourth seal and the fourth living creature says 'Come!', there appears a pale horse whose rider was named Death, with Hades '**following close behind him**'. Hades symbolizes the realm of the dead, the state of disembodied existence.

Whether he makes his mark with a gun in the street, a mine on a battlefield, a terrorist bomb, a plague, an air or rail or road crash, germ warfare, viruses, or just plain 'natural causes', death is always stalking his prey.

The mention of Death and Hades being '**given power over a fourth of the earth**' is a symbolic reminder that these judgements are warnings, rather than God making a full end straight away.

The opening of the fifth seal: the cry of the martyrs

Read verses 9—11 through again. No horses and riders this time, but another abiding sign of the times, another realistic picture of a factor in past, present and future history until Christ returns — the persecution of Christians, even to death. It is clearly they who are spoken of, for John 'saw **under the altar the souls of those who had been slain because of the word of God and the testimony they had maintained'**. The persecution of Christians arises out of the natural man's hatred of God and the gospel. We know only too well how, through history, many have expressed their rejection of the gospel and their despising of the Lord Jesus Christ through hounding, wounding, persecuting and murdering Christians. Jesus laid down a clear principle in His final discourse to His disciples when He warned them, 'If the world hates you, keep in mind that it hated me first . . . If they persecuted me, they will persecute you also . . . They will treat you this way because of my name, for they do not know the One who sent me' (John 15:18—21). But although those Christians John 'saw' were murdered, they were not destroyed. Their enemies had killed their bodies but they could not kill their souls (cf. Matthew 10:28).

Why 'under the altar'? According to the Old Testament book of Leviticus, the blood of slaughtered animals was to be poured out at the base of the altar. The very 'soul' or 'life' was considered to be in the blood. These martyrs sacrificed their lives for the Saviour and His truth and though from the world's side they were hated, from God's point of view their blood was a drink offering poured out to Him, which He highly prized and graciously accepted. Have a look at Paul's testimony in Philippians 2:17. And remember Psalm 116:15: 'Precious in the sight of the Lord is the death of his saints.'

The cry of the martyrs in verse 10 has given rise to some discussion. There are some who are concerned lest it appears to have been uttered in terms of revenge, but that would be to misunderstand it and forget that it is symbolic. They are with Christ, which is far better. All joy is theirs. The Shorter Catechism reminds us that 'The souls of believers are at their death made perfect in holiness and do immediately pass into glory.' Their cry here is not in any conflict with that of Jesus (Luke 23:34) or Stephen (Acts 7:60), for it is not a cry for revenge or retribution as such. What it does express is a deep, passionate and agonizing longing for the day when the church of God will be delivered and triumphant in the face of its enemies, the day when the people of God (and not least the martyrs and their testimony) will be vindicated, and the day, most of all, when God (the '**Sovereign Lord, holy and true**') will be glorified, His kingdom established, His name adored and His will and law no longer flouted. For so long as the Lord of glory tarries and the world continues in unbelief and persecutes the church of God, the holiness and truth of the Saviour will continue by many to be trampled underfoot.

Just notice from verse 11 that the martyrs receive a double satisfaction for their cry. The immediate satisfaction is 'a white robe' for each one. 'Clothed in His righteousness alone, faultless to stand before the throne,' sings out the hymn-writer Edward Mote. The future satisfaction promised is a day for which they must wait patiently, when the number of Christians who are to be sheep for the slaughter will be complete. Then the Lord will return. Then He will judge His enemies. Then He will vindicate and glorify His name. But it is still 'a little longer' that we must wait.

The opening of the first seal: the rider on the white horse

Go back to verses 1–2 and read them through again. The seals have revealed a grim picture so far – war, famine, death and persecution. A realistic picture too, but not the whole picture! Look back to the opening of the first seal by the Lord Jesus Christ. Out came a white horse, upon which was a rider holding a bow and given a crown, '**and he rode out as a conqueror bent on conquest**'.

Some have interpreted the rider as being Christ Himself. I do not think that is correct, despite certain similarities with part of chapter 19 where Christ is riding on a white horse. It is the Lord Jesus Christ who opens the seals in chapter 6, rather than Him being pictured in the contents of the seals.

What we do have here, surely, is a picture of the conquering power of the gospel. This is good news! This is the very encouragement we need, especially after the other seals! Reading the newspapers or watching the news on television you will have constant evidence presented of the second, third, fourth and fifth seals, but little mention of the first. To be sure, you will hear endlessly of the Roman Catholic church and its pope, of the pomp and ceremony of the Church of England and its archbishops and bishops, of various ecumenical efforts and inter-faith services, and all the rest — but not the conquering power of the true gospel. But it is happening! The bow which the rider of the white horse holds fires arrows that strike deep into the hearts of the enemies of the King of kings — sometimes an arrow which carries 'the smell of death', sometimes 'the fragrance of life' (2 Corinthians 2:16). The crown he is given speaks of the victory wreath and is the token of sure success. The manner of the rider is of 'a conqueror bent on conquest' — not someone pussyfooting around in bedroom slippers, but one who knows no defeat, for victory is his work.

We can sum up the key applications so far in three brief imperatives.

Be informed! Read your newspaper in the light of your Bible and do not be one of those who go around apologetically and despairingly moaning, 'I don't know what the world's coming to!'

Be encouraged! Think carefully about the rider on the white horse. Have you got a mighty confidence in the gospel, that 'it is the power of God for the salvation of everyone who believes'? (Romans 1:16.) Are you using those spiritual weapons which 'have divine power to demolish strongholds'? (2 Corinthians 10:4.) Are you looking forward without doubting to that time when 'the earth will be filled with the knowledge of the glory of the Lord, as the waters cover the sea'? (Habakkuk 2:14.) You who preach, realize afresh that promise of God about His Word that goes forth from His mouth: 'It will not return to me empty, but will accomplish what I desire, and achieve the purpose for which I sent it' (Isaiah 55:11). And all dear Christian friends, take to heart the apostle's exhortation: 'Therefore, my dear brothers, stand firm. Let nothing move you. Always give yourselves fully to the work of the Lord, because you know that your labour in the Lord is not in vain' (1 Corinthians 15:58).

Be challenged! Think again about that fifth seal and ask yourself two straight questions. How costly is my commitment to the Lord Jesus Christ? And how burdened am I for the Lord's name and cause?

8.
Sealed and saved

Please read Revelation 6:12—7:17

Two very starkly contrasting sections stand side by side together here. First the Lord Jesus Christ opens the sixth seal (6:12—17), the terrifying contents of which revolve around 'the wrath of the Lamb' (6:16). And following this is the whole of chapter 7, a section which is neither a continuation of the sixth seal nor the opening of the seventh seal (which must wait until 8:1). It is an important and instructive interlude between the two and revolves around 'the blood of the Lamb' (7:14). We can summarize the whole section by saying that it comprises a desperate question and a decisive answer.

1. A desperate question (6:12—17)

These verses bring us closer than we have been so far in the book of Revelation to the second coming of the Lord Jesus Christ. That glorious event is not actually announced or recorded at this point, but we are brought to the very brink of it — as near as possible without actually being there! For what the contents of the sixth seal reveal is the great catastrophe which is coming at the end of the age. And we are left in no doubt that in many vital respects that will be a terrible day, a cataclysmic day, a day which will shake the whole of the universe and everyone in it to their very roots. Three important features stand out for us to notice.

The happenings associated with that day
The details of verses 12—14 add up to nothing less than a

shake-up of the entire physical universe. Can you imagine what it will be like, with a great earthquake, the sun turning black and the moon blood-red, and stars falling from the sky just like fruit falls from the branches of a tree to the ground when shaken by strong winds? And the sky just rolling up like a scroll and the mountains and islands being uprooted and heaved about — can you visualize that?

Some have questioned just how literally we are to take these verses, or even whether we are to take them literally at all. Notwithstanding my repeated insistence that the teaching of Revelation is bound up in symbols and pictures and visual aids, and that every single detail is most certainly not to be taken literally, yet we must be ready to discern when the literal interpretation is the correct one. This is surely such an instance. I agree with Hoeksema when he says, 'Here the literal interpretation is the only explanation possible.'[18] The testimony of other parts of Scripture confirms this. Take time now to look up the following passages from both Testaments: Joel 2:10—11, 30—31; Zephaniah 1:14—18; Haggai 2:6—7; Matthew 24:29—31; 2 Peter 3:7, 10—13. From this comparison it must be emphasized that the contents of the sixth seal reveal the literal dismantling and destruction of the entire physical universe that will be part and parcel of what happens when the Lord in glory comes. As to how precisely it will be 'stage-managed', we must reverently leave that with God. He will perform what He will perform in His own way. But we are in no uncertainty that He will perform it.

But another observation needs to be made. As with the other seals and their contents, so here: there is a present reference to things which are in measure recurring happenings. Earthquakes form a fairly regular item in our news bulletins and, while the worst ones seem usually to be in fairly far away places, from time to time (and especially more recently) tremors and quakes of varying strengths are registered in our own country.

In New Testament times there was an earthquake just after the Lord Jesus Christ was crucified (Matthew 27:51) and Paul and Silas were delivered from prison with the aid of one (Acts 16:26). The darkening of the sun and moon is not a totally strange thing either. Hoeksema draws our attention to the fact that besides periodic eclipses of these heavenly bodies there have been occasions when very strange and unexpected things have happened. One such day occurred in north-east America back in 1780, when it became so dark that it has gone down in history as a supernatural event. Then the stars are mentioned. In 1872 astronomical observers counted as many as 10,000 shooting stars (meteors) falling within two hours, and on another occasion when something similar happened people were thrown into panic and began to cry out to God. And at different points in history, even, mountains have exploded and been blown to pieces, while islands have literally disappeared, such that if you consulted an atlas from some time back some features on it then could no longer be found.

And what is the point of all these interventions by God? They are warnings of the judgement to come, they are given to lead men to repentance and they are designed to impress upon us that there is no security at all in the seeming stability of the world. It is reserved for destruction. It is passing away. Yet none of these 'mini-judgements' (if we dare call them that) can begin to compare with the appalling events of the Day itself.

The people involved in that day
The short answer is everyone! There is an amazingly broad sweep about the people mentioned in verse 15 — people who, for one reason or another, would never think of themselves being thrown together. It amounts to a picture of the entire godless world seized with fear.

Who will be affected? Who will be involved? There will be those of royal blood who have ruled the nations of the world ('**kings**' and '**princes**'); all the military strategists and experts, the battle leaders and the war heroes ('**generals**') will be there. Then there will be those who have had all that the world can offer in terms of its goods and influence ('**the rich**' and '**the mighty**'), along with those who have been considered to be the very scum and off-scouring of society and who have often been most shamefully treated and thrown around ('**slaves**'). There too will be all the democrats and free citizens, all those who have prized and fought for liberty, all who have 'done their own thing' and have felt answerable to no one ('every free man'). And what do they all have in common? How is it that such a diverse company can be brought together? What is it that will level them all in the end? Quite simply this: they rejected the Lord Jesus Christ.

There is no security at all in the seeming stability offered either by exalted position or lowly position in life — in either pressing on up the ladder or, as some do, opting out of society altogether.

The cry heard on that day

We often speak of trying to imagine the sight of things in our 'mind's eye'. If we may coin a new expression, we need to imagine also the sound of things in our 'mind's ear'! Especially is this so as we look at verses 15–17.

Here are two of the most terrible verses in the New Testament. The whole array of people we have just described are seen here desperately trying to take cover, in a panic to find some hiding place. They run to the caves, they crouch behind rocks, but nowhere can they find a place to get out of the sight of the coming glorious Lord Jesus Christ. Can you hear the swearing, the wailing, the weeping and the cursing? Maybe you have seen those terrible scenes on television news bulletins after a bomb has gone off in an airport, for example, and everyone is scrambling for their life, shrieking and shouting. Complete pandemonium breaks out. Perhaps that gives us something like a millionth of a millionth idea of what it will be like on the great and terrible day of the Lord.

Can you imagine, in your right mind, calling on a mountain or a great rock to drop on you? Yet even the thought of that will be preferable and more comfortable on the last day when compared with the thought of having to face — naked, helpless, ashamed and without any excuse — 'him who sits on the throne and . . . the wrath of the Lamb'. Not even the proudest, most boastful or most stout-hearted sinner will be able to stand.

There is no security to be found anywhere in the whole of creation. 'For the great day of their wrath has come, and who can stand?'

2. A decisive answer (7:1–17)

With that terrible cliff-hanger question still ringing in our ears, we come to chapter 7. What can the answer be to 6:17? Who can stand? Can anybody stand?

I asked you earlier to look up the prophecy of Joel in Joel 2, and that prophecy continues with 2:32 – and how thankful we are that it does!

> 'And everyone who calls
>   on the name of the Lord will be saved;
> for on Mount Zion and in Jerusalem
>   there will be deliverance,
>   as the Lord has said,
> among the survivors
>   whom the Lord calls.'

Notice those two vital phrases: 'everyone who calls on the name of the Lord' and 'whom the Lord calls'.

In line with this, the answer to the question chapter 6 left us with comes ringing back in chapter 7 like this: the servants of God who have the seal of the living God upon their foreheads (2–3), '144,000 from all the tribes of Israel' (4), 'a great multitude that no one could count, from every nation, tribe, people and language' (9), and, most specifically and gloriously of all, those who 'have washed their robes and made them white in the blood of the Lamb' (14). They are the ones who will stand! They are secure! They have no cause to fear!

John has a fresh vision. 'After this I saw . . . ,' he says in verse 1. Let us ask four basic questions about these people who will stand, in order to draw out the teaching of this chapter.

Who are they?
We have just noticed that they are described four times in this chapter. Look at those descriptions again – from verses 2–3, 4, 9 and 14.

They are *the sealed servants of God* (2–3). The seal in the Bible is the mark of God's ownership and God's protection. It is not a literal mark upon the forehead, but a reminder that 'The Lord knows those who are his' (2 Timothy 2:19). His children are marked ones, certified as being His, preserved as His. For He has chosen us before the foundation of the world, set His love upon us, made us His own and will never let us go.

The chapter opens with John seeing **'four angels standing at the four corners of the earth, holding back the four winds of the earth to prevent any wind from blowing on the land or on the sea or on any tree'** (1). 'Winds here mean not the gentle and refreshing breezes, but the hurricanes that sweep all before them with ruin and spread complete destruction in their path. They represent all the violent and resistless powers and influences which, when let loose, are to sweep over the earth, and involve it in the ruin just depicted in the previous scene.'[19] But then John sees **'another angel . . .'** (2) who called out in a loud voice a message to these first four angels: **'Do not harm the land or the sea or the trees until we put a seal on the foreheads of the servants of our God'** (3). There you have it! The woes of God are punishments for the wicked, persecuting, unbelieving world. The upheavals of the world, both as the world goes along on its course and then supremely at the Last Day, cannot ultimately harm the people of God, for He has sealed us as His very own possession.

This sealing is pictured in terms of *the tribes of Israel* (4–8), but this is not speaking of Israel as a nation but the true Israel, the spiritual Israel, the church, described by the apostle Paul as 'the Israel of God' (Galatians 6:16). The number 144,000 is not to be taken literally. It occurs again in 14:1 and stands symbolically for all those from the Old and New Testament dispensations who belong to God through faith in the Lord Jesus Christ.

They comprise *an innumerable company* (9). There is no contradiction between this and the symbolic use of 144,000. The company of God's elect is a fixed number (He knows exactly whom He has chosen), so that in that sense 144,000 is symbolic of a fixed number, while still not itself being the actual number. But the elect are quite beyond the possibility of man ever counting them. It reminds us of God's word to Abraham about the sand and the stars (Genesis 15:5; 22:17). And regarding the universality of where the elect are drawn from, remember the Saviour's great commission, which He issued to His church before He ascended into heaven: 'Go and make disciples of all nations' (Matthew 28:19). 'Go into all the world and preach the good news to all creation' (Mark 16:15).

But it is *the description given in verse 14* that is the high point. Blood usually causes a stain, and one which can be very hard (sometimes impossible) to remove. But the blood of the Lord Jesus Christ gloriously removes the deeply-dyed stains of our sins. His blood speaks of His death upon the cross at Calvary for sinners. Imagine taking a robe, drenching it in blood, and then finding it comes out white! Yet that is what happens when we trust in Christ as our Saviour! It is the truth of Isaiah 1:18. *Only the blood of the Lamb can shield us from the wrath of the Lamb.*

> There is a fountain filled with blood,
> Drawn from Immanuel's veins;
> And sinners plunged beneath that flood
> Lose all their guilty stains
> (William Cowper).

Where are they?
The answer is given in verse 9b: '**standing before the throne and in front of the Lamb**'. Nothing remains now to separate them from God or to disqualify them from His presence. Christ has died for them — God has accepted Christ's work and accepted them in Christ — and in Him they possess all things for life and for eternity.

The reference in verse 14 to them having '**come out of the great tribulation**' is not to be taken as a reference to some particular event around the end time, but rather an assertion that Christ has made them victorious and brought them safe through all their afflictions and trials to glory. Has He not promised that He will not lose a single one of all those whom the Father has given to Him? (John 6:39.) So Toplady can rejoice and so can we:

> Safe in the arms of sovereign love
>> We ever shall remain;
> Nor shall the rage of earth or hell
>> Make Thy sure counsel vain.
> Not one of all the chosen race
>> But shall to heaven attain;
> Here they will share abounding grace,
>> And there with Jesus reign.

What are they doing?

Rejoicing in their God-given standing and praising their Redeemer — that's what they are doing! Just look at verses 9c–12 and see! The angels are there and the four living creatures are there and a magnificent paean of praise to God bursts forth. The song **'Salvation belongs to our God . . .'** (10) means that salvation proceeds from God, it is His work and so all honour and praise are due to Him alone for it. Hendriksen observes that the definite article precedes each of the seven items of praise in the doxology of verse 12 (the praise, the glory, the wisdom, etc.) and remarks, 'It indicates that in the fullest, deepest sense these excellences pertain to God, and to Him alone.'

This time it is Fanny J. Crosby who has the appropriate lines:

> Blessed assurance, Jesus is mine!
>> Oh, what a foretaste of glory divine!
> Heir of salvation, purchase of God;
>> Born of His Spirit, washed in His blood.
>
> This is my story, this is my song,
> Praising my Saviour all the day long.

How are they living?

Do you think much of heaven? The final verses of this chapter (15–17) are some of the most exquisite not only in the book of Revelation, but in the whole of the Bible. In a wonderfully full and suggestive way they set forth 'life in heaven'. What will that life be like? It will be a life of unwearied service (15a), unbounded security (15b–16) and unblemished satisfaction (16–17).

A life of unwearied service. We are accustomed to speak of 'the heavenly rest', and that is right and biblical. But it is not the rest of going to sleep and never waking up, the rest of idleness or sloth, or the rest of retirement or loafing about. Far from it — we shall be busy in heaven! We shall rest from all the labours and trials and struggles with in-dwelling sin which have been so much part of our life on earth, but we shall still have plenty to do.

We shall be '**before the throne of God**'. That throne will be the centre-piece or focal point of heaven. Our whole life will be lived in relation to it and the One who sits upon it. The preposition 'before' is significant. It speaks of full and intimate fellowship, with no sense for us of being at a distance from God, even in that numberless throng! And we shall '**serve him day and night in his temple**'. The whole of heaven, the whole of God's new creation, will be His temple, where He dwells. All the redeemed and all the redeemed creation will glorify Him. We shall walk constantly and unbrokenly in His presence, serving Him day and night without any weariness, staleness or weakness.

We cannot very easily enlarge upon the nature of that service, except to say that at its heart will be worship and praise. We shall never before have been so happy in any employment!

A life of unbounded security. Two wonderful expressions are used to draw this out. We shall be covered by God's tent — what a picture of the enjoyment of the warmth of God's love and the delights of His presence! Then shall we know the full meaning of being taken into His banqueting hall, with His banner of love over us (Song of Songs 2:4). And we shall be kept by God's power. We love the sun, especially when we are on holiday. But too much sun can cause us trouble! But not in heaven! No harm will come near us, nothing will hurt us or cause us to be afraid, no trouble will be anywhere in sight, no old sins will rise up to torment us and no more will there by any suffering for the precious name of Jesus. Instead, the glory of the Lord will shine upon us — yet even that, the full sight of which we could not at present bear, will not consume us in its heat or blind us in its dazzling power.

A life of unblemished satisfaction. And that satisfaction will be pre-eminently in the Lamb. We shall enjoy God's provision — nothing will make us hungry or thirsty any more. There will never be any sense of 'something missing'. We shall have everything we desire and desire everything we have. Our bodies will be glorified and perfected, our sins will be stamped out for ever, our hearts will be fixed upon Him in whose heaven we dwell and our company will be Christ Himself and all the saints.

We shall be shepherded by the Lamb. There is something remarkable here. The Lord Jesus Christ is both the Lamb and the Shepherd. As the Lamb of God who was slain, He bought us with His blood. As the Shepherd who supplies all our needs, He will look after us in every way imaginable. Water, in Scripture, regularly symbolizes eternal life and salvation, and the fact that the Lord Jesus Christ will lead us **'to springs of living water'** reminds us that in heaven we shall be at the very source and focus of spiritual life and blessing.

And we shall be delivered from all sorrow. Here on earth our joys are often tempered by our sorrows. We are no strangers to the vale of tears. But our God will not only deliver us from all actual sorrow, but even from the very possibility of it, for the tears will be wiped not just 'from' but right 'out of' our eyes!

How wonderful it will be to be a citizen of heaven! Are you already one right now? If you are, then already you have begun to live a life in God's service, a life surrounded by God's security and a life replete with God's satisfactions — but the best is still yet to be!

There is a lovely old hymn which, because it takes up the thoughts of these closing verses of chapter 7 so beautifully, and because it is not readily to be found in hymn-books, would be worth printing here in full for our meditation and to draw out our hearts in worship to our glorious God of grace!

What will it be to dwell above,
   And with the Lord of glory reign,
Since the sweet earnest of His love
   So brightens all this dreary plain?
No heart can think, no tongue explain
What joy 'twill be with Christ to reign.

When sin no more obstructs our sight,
   When sorrow pains the heart no more,
When we shall see the Prince of light,
   And all His works of grace explore,
What heights and depths of love divine
Will there through endless ages shine!

Our God has fixed the happy day
   When the last tear shall dim our eyes,
When He will wipe all tears away,
   And fill our hearts with glad surprise,
To hear His voice, to see His face,
And know the riches of His grace.

This is the joy we seek to know,
   For this with patience we would wait,
Till called from earth and all below,
   We rise, our gracious Lord to meet;
To wave our palm, our crown to wear,
And praise the love that brought us there.[20]

9.
The seven trumpets

Please read Revelation 8 and 9

Chapter 7, as I said earlier, was an interlude, though a glorious one! The sixth seal was opened at the end of chapter 6, and its contents took us to the very eve of the final judgement. Now in 8:1 the Lord Jesus Christ opens the seventh and final seal — yet does not the result surprise you? **'When he opened the seventh seal, there was silence in heaven for about half an hour.'**

Hosts of interpretations have been given of that half-hour silence. Some may be right, some may be wrong; we are certainly not going to stop and weigh them all up! Comparing Scripture with Scripture, it is best interpreted as *a silence of awe before God*, along the lines of Habakkuk 2:20 and the summons there: 'The Lord is in his holy temple; let all the earth be silent before him.' It is also *a silence of peace before God*, for no one had any grounds for complaint as the Lord had silenced all opposition, and it has become clear at last that the Judge of all the earth has done right. And it is *a silence of expectation before God*, preparing us for the terrible character of the judgements that are still to be related. This last is particularly so because now that the seven seals have all been opened, we are led to another series of seven related happenings (see 8:2 and 8:6), which comprise warnings of God's judgements upon an impenitent earth, under the figure of the blowing of seven trumpets. The trumpets are synchronous with the seals, and like them refer to events which span the whole of history and especially the period from the first to the second coming of Christ.

But before we come to the trumpets in detail, just observe the little section 8:3—5, from which we may glean:

Three primary principles about prayer

These can be summarized quite briefly in this way:

1. God's people are given the great privilege of prayer
The subject of this small section is **'the prayers of all the saints'** (3). Some people make the serious mistake of making 'saints' of certain specially selected dead people, while the Bible teaches us clearly that saints are very much alive! 'Saints' is one of the New Testament's descriptions for Christians (have a look at Romans 1:7 and Philippians 1:1, then 1 Corinthians 1:2). And prayer should occupy a place right at the very heart of the Christian life. It is a Calvary-bought privilege. We have access into God's holy presence to pray through the merits and death of the Lord Jesus Christ — otherwise we could not come at all.

The Shorter Catechism has a helpful summary statement about prayer: 'Prayer is an offering up of our desires unto God, for things agreeable to His will, in the name of Christ, with confession of our sins, and thankful acknowledgement of His mercies.' And in a lovely section of his highly recommended book on prayer, Guy Appéré speaks about the three aspects of our relationship to God in prayer: we come as the creature before the Creator, the sinner before the just and holy God and the son before the Father.[21]

2. God's people are promised great assistance in prayer
Look at verses 3–4 and see what happened. Some have been very keen to identify the altar. Is it the altar of incense, since incense is mentioned? Or is it the altar of burnt offering, as smoke and fire are mentioned? But there is no need to ask the question. The whole is symbolic and the great idea here, which we miss if we try to be finnicky about the identity of the altar, is this: the prayers of all the saints rise up before God and are made acceptable to God, well-pleasing in His sight and agreeable to His will.

According to the symbolism it is the application of the incense which makes the prayers fit and suitable to be presented to God. Going behind the symbolism, Scripture shows us that there are two great assistances promised to every believer in order that we may pray aright, and both

are mentioned in Romans 8: the intercession of the Holy
Spirit (Romans 8:26–27) and the intercession of the Lord
Jesus Christ (Romans 8:34). James Montgomery puts it all
together in these lines:

> No prayer is made on earth alone,
>   The Holy Spirit pleads,
> And Jesus, on the eternal throne,
>   For sinners intercedes.

What marvellous news!

3. God's people are guaranteed great answers to prayer
'Guaranteed' is not an over-statement or a presumption,
though it is important to add that our prayers must be
motivated by a desire for God's own glory, and they must
be agreeable to His will.

Commenting upon verse 5, the writer in Matthew Henry's
commentary remarks, 'These prayers that were thus accepted
in heaven produced great changes upon earth in return to
them . . . these were the answers God gave to the prayers
of the saints.' If you reply, 'Yes, but the answers surely
were tokens of His anger against the world' ('**and there
came peals of thunder, rumblings, flashes of lightning and
an earthquake**'), then remember that when we are pleading
with God that He would vindicate His name and cause,
avenge Himself against His enemies, glorify His saints and
bring in His kingdom, then such answers must be expected.
That is a great part of what the seals, trumpets and bowls
are all about and so why 8:3–5 appears at this point in
the book of Revelation. Remember Proverbs 15:8: 'The
prayer of the upright pleases him.' Our God is the prayer-
hearing and prayer-answering God!

The seven trumpets

And so we come to the seven trumpets themselves. Let us
look at them one by one. As was the pattern with the seals,
the first four trumpets are very clearly related (8:6–13)
and there is another interlude between the sixth and seventh

(10:1—11:14). It is worth reiterating one more time the principle of progressive parallelism: the trumpets, like the seals, relate to God's constant and continuing operations in the world that He has made and rules, while the judgements represented by them become more emphatic and more severe as the time draws near for the coming of the Lord Jesus Christ. The language in which the judgements here are expressed reminds us of the ten plagues in Egypt in the book of Exodus.

The first trumpet (8:7)
All of the first four trumpets refer to the visible universe and each trumpet in John's vision is blown by an angel. First of all, tremendous storms of hail and fire mixed with blood are pictured being hurled down upon the earth — stones which, not surprisingly, have great destructive power on the earth itself, the trees and the grass (notice even the detail of 'green' grass). This presents us with a picture of calamities to the earth and its vegetation, sent by God as instruments to warn and to punish the wicked: crops ruined; trees, grass and herbs destroyed; the environment spoiled. The phrase 'hurled down upon the earth' indicates that these calamities are controlled in heaven, and the fraction of one-third speaks of a hotting-up of things (under the seals the fraction was one quarter).

The second trumpet (8:8—9)
This time the sea rather than the land is on the receiving end of various calamities. John sees not an actual mountain but 'something like a huge mountain, all ablaze', thrown into the sea, with great trouble and commotion resulting. This would include sweeping tempests, death of fish and other creatures of the sea and the loss of ships (along with their passengers and crews) and the toppling of oil-rig platforms. 'If the loss of lives and properties in all sea disasters throughout history could be calculated, this vision would not seem at all extravagant.'[22]

The third trumpet (8:10—11)
So far the land and the sea have been mentioned. Now it is the turn of the inland waterways (rivers, springs, canals,

reservoirs and so on). Again the vision presents a frightening picture. What is meant by the star called 'Wormwood'? Is it meant to symbolize an actual star, shattered to pieces and strewn on the waters? Or is it a comet leaving behind its poisonous gases? The word 'Wormwood' means bitter sorrow and is taken from the name of a plant noted for its very bitter taste. Whatever precisely is meant by the star, its effects will fill the hearts of men with awful sorrow. Waters will be poisoned and polluted. People will die through drinking them. Industry and commerce will be affected.

The fourth trumpet (8:12)

This one is a little more difficult to interpret, but it seems to speak of abnormal functioning in the heavenly bodies (sun, moon and stars), with less sunshine, periods of strange darkness and stars shining less brightly — all of which should make people question and fear, but more importantly, seek the Lord! When will people take God seriously?

Then the eagle — a bird of prey in a suitable role — soars aloft with its message of further woes to come (8:13). Things are not finished yet!

The fifth trumpet (9:1–12)

The descriptions of the fifth and sixth trumpets are longer and more detailed than the preceding ones. As soon as the fifth angel sounded his trumpet, John 'saw a star that had fallen from the sky to the earth'. We must take that in the light of the Saviour's words: 'I saw Satan fall like lightning from heaven' (Luke 10:18). As John's vision continues, the star (either Satan or one of his minions) was given the key to the shaft of the Abyss. Wilson defines 'the Abyss' as 'the abode of demons before the final judgement and the reservoir of evil from which the worst dangers arise,' while Hendriksen calls it 'hell before the final judgement'.

When the Abyss was opened, two things happened: terrible smoke belched out, darkening sun and sky, and then out of this smoke came a great army of locusts. They are described symbolically in verses 7–10, and according to verse 11 have a king whose name both in Hebrew (Abaddon) and Greek (Apollyon) means 'destroyer'. Looking back to verses 4–6, we have an alarming picture of their work: they are concerned to do all the harm they can to all who do not have God's seal upon their foreheads, and that will include torturing them and tormenting them for a set time (the five months is symbolic for a limited period — compare the ten days of 2:10), though not killing them.

Actual locusts are terrible destroyers — refresh your memory of the descriptions given in Exodus 10:4—15 and Joel 2:2—11. But these locusts before us under the vision of the fifth trumpet are neither literal locusts nor are they symbolic of men. They are fallen, evil, demonic angels (cf. 2 Peter 2:4 and Jude 6), whom Hoeksema describes variously as 'the reserve troops of hell', Satan's 'special forces' or 'an infernal army of demons let loose by Satan for a definite purpose'. When Satan fell, he did not fall alone. We do not know how many angels fell with him, after the failure of the rebellion in heaven, but the impression Scripture gives us is of a vast number. They have not yet received their final judgement or punishment; that will take place on the Last Day, when they will all be thrown into the lake of fire prepared especially for them (20:10; cf. Matthew 25:41). But until then, just as Satan is prowling around like a roaring lion, so they too are far from inactive!

At one point (10) their torment is likened to a scorpion sting, which does not actually kill but causes such agony and misery that a person longs to be dead. Chronic hardships that bring terrible times but not utter ruin, terrible diseases that cripple but do not kill, beckoning philosophies that offer the fleeting pleasures of sin but leave a nasty taste and an aching void, temptations to ambition and success which excite people and deliver temporary happiness before leaving folk dangling, dissatisfied and bitter, casting them into pessimism and despair, leading them 'up the garden path' — these are some of the effects of the contents of the fifth trumpet. And while many would long to commit suicide (6) to be free of it all, their courage fails them. What a picture of the most appalling gloom and misery!

Then another 'woe' (12) and on to the sixth trumpet.

The sixth trumpet (9:13—21)
The alarming vision John is being given continues with this picture of four angels ready to plunge mankind into

war, leading to a view of armies on the field of battle
numbering (symbolically again) 200 million! The picture
of them in verses 17–19 (one of fury, terror and power)
speaks for itself, leading to widespread death and injury.

Here is a picture of war — not any one particular war
but war itself, past, present and future. What a terrible
evil war is! And all the picture of the **'horses and riders'**
reminds us of the building up of war machinery and military
arsenals — something which we see in unparalleled measure
in our own day, with talk even of war in outer space with
'star wars' technology and weapons.

All in all, these six trumpets do not paint a very pretty
picture. The seventh trumpet is blown in 11:15. But before
we go into the interlude, it is necessary to gather up some
of the leading lines of application so far. We can summarize
them like this:

*Only the Bible gives us the right key to interpret events of
history.* While the Bible is concerned supremely with
declaring God's great plan of salvation, it is far more than a
place to come to just to get our evangelistic proof texts.
It is a book for the whole of life and which interprets the
whole of history, not just a handbook for personal salvation
and sanctification.

The terrible power of evil and error. Sin, the flesh, the
false ideas of man, war and such like are often glorified, in
books and films, for example. But the reality is that people
who trifle with the truth, play with sin and openly pursue
evil themselves and lead others to do the same are utterly
blinded and under the grip of darkness. Not without good
reason is the devil described in Scripture as 'the ruler of the
kingdom of the air' and his armies as 'the spiritual forces
of evil in the heavenly realms'. And remember that the
most successful of all his tricks is to persuade people either
that he does not exist or else that he does not need to be
taken seriously.

The appalling depravity of the human heart. Jeremiah in
no way overstates the case when he observes that 'The
heart is deceitful above all things and beyond cure. Who can

understand it?' (Jeremiah 17:9.) We noticed that one of the chief reasons for the trumpets was that they might serve as warnings from God to unbelieving sinners, that they might turn from their evil ways and seek the Lord. But, by and large, do they? Look at 9:20—21, with its picture not of a generally repentant world but an increasingly hardened world. Still both tables of God's law are broken (verse 20 shows the rejection of the first four commandments, and verse 21 does the same for the remaining six). Wickedness flourishes.

The amazing longsuffering and patience of God towards rebel sinners. How beyond our comprehension it is that God does not just go ahead and make a full end of judgement straight away! But still He warns. Still the gospel is preached. Still sinners are exhorted 'that they must turn to God in repentance and have faith in our Lord Jesus' (Acts 20:21). It can only be explained by the fact that He is 'a gracious and compassionate God, slow to anger and abounding in love, a God who relents from sending calamity' (Jonah 4:2). But sinners' continued refusal to repent will eventually bring in the last, the final, judgement. God's patience will end. The day of grace will be over. The door to life will be shut for ever.

The glorious assurance for those who belong to the Lord. There is no need for believers to be afraid. We have God's seal of ownership and protection upon us. The things revealed as the trumpets are blown must come to pass, and they will do so even more forcefully and plainly as the days go on. But still we need not be afraid. For even though Christians will inevitably be touched by these happenings (a major crop failure, for example, can affect us all, and who knows what 'disasters' any of us may be involved in?), yet remember this: the spiritual kingdom of Christ is invulnerable. Our life is now hidden with Christ in God.

10.
The angel and the little scroll

Please read Revelation 10

A mighty angel coming down from heaven and the apostle John eating a little scroll — these are the two 'scenes' of chapter 10 of the book of Revelation which commences the interlude between the blowing of the sixth and seventh trumpets of warning. Like the earlier interlude in chapter 7, this one is full of Christ and full of rich spiritual material.

1. Things revealed and things kept hidden

Two vital aspects of God's character and ways are set forth in verses 1—7.

The God who makes himself known (1—2)
A question right at the start which has puzzled students of this passage is whether the angel whom John saw in this vision is actually the Lord Jesus Christ or not. Some say, 'yes', some say, 'no' and some reserve their position and say nothing at all! The judgement to which I incline is that the angel is not strictly and actually Christ Himself appearing, for he is described as 'another mighty angel', which is a fairly indefinite description. Further, Christ is not any-where plainly called an angel in Revelation, and we do not read in this chapter that John worshipped the angel as in chapter 1 he had worshipped Christ. But, while we hold all this in mind, the characteristics and attributes ascribed to the angel are so ascribed in order to direct us to what God is like — the God who makes Himself known, the God who does not remain hidden so that we should never

know anything about Him, the God moreover who has 'made his light shine in our hearts to give us the light of the knowledge of the glory of God in the face of Christ' (2 Corinthians 4:6).

He is the God who reveals Himself, tells us what He is like and, most wonderful of all, even brings us into a personal relationship with Him. 'Now this is eternal life: that they may know you, the only true God, and Jesus Christ, whom you have sent' (John 17:3).

What is your view of God? Look at some of the details here. Follow them through and see what they reveal.

1. 'Robed in a cloud' (1). So often in the Bible the cloud is the symbol of divine majesty, and in particular His majesty coming for judgement (cf. Psalm 97:2; Mark 13:26). Our God, our Christ, is not someone who can be run away from or bypassed for ever.

2. 'With a rainbow above his head'. As we noticed from 4:3, ever since God's dealings with Noah the rainbow has been the symbol of divine grace, mercy and faithfulness. The hymn-writer J. F. Webb puts it like this:

> God of the covenant, triune Jehovah,
> Marvels of mercy adoring we see;
> Seeker of souls, in the counsels eternal
> Binding Thy lost ones for ever to Thee.

3. 'His face was like the sun.' Here is a reminder once more of God's holiness and glory, which would be too great for mortal eyes to look upon if it was left unveiled. Do you remember the transfiguration of the Lord Jesus Christ, how then 'his face shone like the sun'? (Matthew 17:2.) When recalling that later on, the apostle Peter wrote, 'We were eye-witnesses of his majesty' (2 Peter 1:16).

4. 'His legs were like fiery pillars.' This is a symbol both of God's strength and the firmness and stability of all his ways and purposes (cf. Isaiah 46:10).

5. *'His posture'* (2). What is meant by the angel having one foot on the sea and one foot on the land? Precisely this: our God, our Saviour, rules the world and His message must be published to all! Answer quite frankly: who do you think rules the world? The devil? The British Government,

Opposition and SDP-Liberal alliance between them? The President of the United States? The leaders of the Soviet Union? The trade unions? The terrorists? The oil sheiks? The pope? None of them! None of them!

This symbol of the angel's posture speaks of the absolute power and dominion which God exercises over the world. In the Bible, if you place your foot on something then it is symbolic of subjection and possession. Examples may be found in Joshua 10:24; Psalm 110:1; 1 Corinthians 15: 25, Ephesians 1:22 and other places. And as the angel **'planted his right foot on the sea and his left foot on the land'**, nothing is left out. God alone is the Ruler and Possessor of all things. It may appear sometimes as if they belong to someone else because of the pride and ambition of men and the spread and grip of sin and godlessness, but no! They belong to Him! And the day will come when this will be seen to be so. But it is so right now, at this very moment.

There is wonderful comfort here for the Christian. Nothing happens, whether on the level of global affairs, national and international events, or in the sphere of our own little lives, which alters in any way the sovereign sway of God, the sovereign sway of the Lord Jesus Christ, to whom 'all authority in heaven and on earth has been given' (Matthew 28:18). Our fears, doubts and anxieties need to be dispelled, for they cast dishonour upon the name of our God. He is to be trusted and relied upon. He is constantly at work. He can never fail.

The God who keeps his secrets (3–7)
The angel planted his feet, he roared like a lion, **'the voices of the seven thunders spoke'** (3), and John was just about to write down what they said when he was commanded by a voice from heaven not to.

Just as God makes Himself known, so also when He is pleased to do so He keeps His secrets. There is no possible way we can find out what the thunders said; it is a locked-away secret. It is a mystery. And here we should be brought to the place where we are humbled under the mighty hand of God. In getting hold of this principle, verses like Psalm

77:19 and Isaiah 45:15 are important, but none more so than Deuteronomy 29:29, where you have the whole of the matter in perfect balance: 'The secret things belong to the Lord our God, but the things revealed belong to us and to our children for ever, that we may follow all the words of this law.'

Not everything about God's character, purposes and ways can be known. Sometimes the way of His working appears to be mysterious and incomprehensible. There are and will continue to be many things we are not able to look into or explain. But our reaction to that should not be to question God on these matters, still less to doubt God or to accuse Him. Rather should we praise Him for His graciousness in being pleased to reveal so much to us (this very book is Revelation!) and await the divine and glorious outcome of world history and our own personal history with holy fear and deep humility. 'We are to be subdued before the vastness of the unknown purposes of God.'[23]

In due time delay will cease (6) and all 'the mystery of God will be accomplished' (7). The day will come — what a day it will be! — when our glorious God will give a full, satisfying and God-glorifying answer to all His children's bewildered questions. Everything will make sense and fall into its place, even His permissions of evil, the apparent prosperity of the wicked and God's perfect purposes in all our trials, afflictions and holy longings. It is a spiritual mark of the true believer that he is willing to wait. Are you willing to wait?

2. The apostle John and the bitter-sweet scroll

I did not comment upon it at the time, but back in verse 2 the angel is pictured 'holding a little scroll, which lay open in his hand'. In verse 8 John is directed by the same voice from heaven that he had already heard to do two things: first to take the scroll from the angel and then to eat it. He was told that it would taste as sweet as honey in his mouth but would be very sour or bitter in his stomach. So he did exactly as he was instructed and found the effect of eating the scroll to be exactly as he had been told (9—10).

He then received the command to prophesy (11). Do remember that all this is still symbolic — John saw it in a vision.

We need to know the answers to three questions in order to understand and apply this passage: What is the little scroll? What is signified by John eating the scroll? What is the meaning of the sweet and sour effects?

What is the little scroll?

This is not hard to discover. From the context itself and from a comparison with clear Scriptures like Psalm 119:103; Jeremiah 15:16 and Ezekiel 2:9–3:4, the scroll is surely the Word of God, the mystery of salvation that is set forth in the gospel and which the sinner first receives and then proclaims and, not least, all the material which John is yet to witness and declare.

Those other verses we have just mentioned really clinch it. The psalmist says about God's Word: 'How sweet are your words to my taste, sweeter than honey to my mouth!' The prophet Jeremiah testifies, 'When your words came, I ate them; they were my joy and my heart's delight.' And the Ezekiel passage, which bears a very strong affinity with our present section in Revelation, also has the prophet eating a scroll upon which is God's message which he has to preach and which tastes as sweet as honey in his mouth.

What is signified by John eating the scroll?

He is told quite specifically, '**Take it and eat it**' (9). To be a Christian and therefore a proclaimer of the Lord Jesus Christ, a merely external relationship with the gospel will not do. It will not avail anything. It is no use being like that man James speaks of who listens to the Word of God but does not do what it says and so 'is like a man who looks at his face in a mirror and, after looking at himself, goes away and immediately forgets what he looks like' (James 1:22–24). He deceives himself! Nor is it any use being like the man Jesus speaks of who 'hears these words of mine and does not put them into practice' and so is like a foolish man who builds a house which falls down because it has no solid foundation (Matthew 7:24–27).

Hearing the gospel, listening to the gospel, sitting under

the preaching of the gospel, knowing all the facts about Jesus, being able to quote the Scriptures and even hold your own in a doctrinal discussion, going through various church ceremonies, being related to greatly used preachers and so on — none of this is sufficient. It is an external relationship only.

What is needed is 'that Christ may dwell in your hearts through faith' (Ephesians 3:17); to know God, to know Christ (John 17:3); to be not just a hearer of the Word but a doer of the Word as well (James 1:22); to, as it were, digest the gospel, have it become a very part of you, as is envisaged in this symbolic eating. The Word of Christ needs to dwell in you deeply and richly (Colossians 3:16). You need to have the gospel — and the Lord Jesus Christ who is Himself the very sum and centre of the gospel — transform you from the inside out, change you, make you a different person, a new creation in Christ (2 Corinthians 5:17).

The great truths of the gospel, such as the mighty facts of the work of Christ dying at Calvary and rising again on the third day, must not be just intellectual curiosities to us. They must take hold of us. They must affect vitally our hearts, minds, consciences, wills and lives — our past, present and future — our priorities, affections, work, relationships — everything about us!

'Take it and eat it' — receive inwardly the gospel and the One of whom it speaks. Be captive to Him.

What is the meaning of the sweet and sour effects?
Every believer surely knows that once you have 'eaten the gospel', in the sense already explained of being embraced and taken over by the Saviour and His Word, there is both sweetness and sourness, to use the senses mentioned here.

The sweetness of receiving the gospel. Our friend John Newton got to the heart of it when he wrote:

> How sweet the name of Jesus sounds
> In a believer's ear!

The gospel itself and the Saviour it proclaims are

indescribably sweet to the taste of faith. To know the delight of your sin being pardoned, being justified before God, adopted as His child, filled with His Holy Spirit, having a glorious and indestructible heavenly hope, fellowship with God — and so much else! — is this not sweet beyond words? 'Now to you who believe [Christ] is precious,' testifies Peter (1 Peter 2:7). 'I delight to sit in his shade, and his fruit is sweet to my taste,' is every believer's testimony concerning Christ (Song of Songs 2:3).

The sourness of receiving the gospel. Yes, there is this side to it as well for the Christian. The same gospel that is so sweet to the taste ('it tasted as sweet as honey in my mouth,' 10) is also sometimes sour as we digest it and work it out in our lives in an ungodly world ('but when I had eaten it, my stomach turned sour,' 10). By this sourness or bitterness, of course, is not meant that the gospel is harmful, that the believer regrets having been brought to the knowledge and possession of it, or anything like that. Rather the emphasis is upon the demanding, self-denying nature of the gospel.

So there is *the continual problem of wrestling with indwelling sin.* One preacher has spoken vividly of the 'bitterness of spiritual sorrow resulting from inwardly digesting the truths of the gospel and bringing them thus into close contact with the secret maladies of the soul'. Then there is also *the self-denial and daily cross-bearing* required of the Christian. The Christian does not live on easy street and just sail through life in a dream! The road, as John Bunyan's Pilgrim found, is often a dark road, a terrible road, a road surrounded by enemies, a costly road.

There is also *the casting off of the gospel* round about us. What a grief this is to the sensitive believer, that the Lord Jesus Christ and the gospel should be treated so lightly and rejected so widely!

But even that is not all. There is the bitterness of *persecution for Christ's sake and the gospel*, which is something, as we have seen, that John himself and many Christians of his day were having to face. There is the difficult, though very necessary, business of *speaking of matters like God's wrath and the everlastingness of hell* to unbelievers. It was especially in the declaring of God's Word to the 'peoples, **nations, languages and kings**' (11) that John experienced the bitterness of the scroll. Upon this, Leon Morris remarks: 'The true preacher of God's Word will faithfully proclaim the denunciations of the wicked it contains. But he does not do this with fierce glee. The more his heart is filled with the love of God the more certain it is that the telling forth of "woes" will be a bitter experience.'[24]

We cannot avoid the question which comes to each one of us. Do you know the sweetness of the gospel? And do you know the sourness of the gospel too? It is time for renewed self-examination. Does the Lord Jesus Christ dwell in and control your life? Can you say, 'My Beloved is mine and I am his'? (Song of Songs 2:16). And are you faithful to Him, ready to spend and be spent for Him and counting all things loss for Him?

11.
A chapter of mysteries

Please read Revelation 11

The interlude between the blowing of the sixth and seventh trumpets continues as we come to chapter 11. This is one of the most important chapters of the entire book, remarks Dr Hoeksema, which is absolutely true. It is also, in my opinion, the most difficult — especially the central section from verses 3—13. As so often with portions of the book of Revelation, endless theories of interpretation have been given and we must be very careful in the conclusions that we come to if we are to divide the Word of truth rightly.

Notice straight away that the chapter falls clearly into three sections:

The measuring of the temple of God (1—2)

The two witnesses (3—13)

The blowing of the seventh trumpet (14—19).

Surely it hardly needs to be said by now that John is receiving all this material in a vision, and so we continue to be faced with symbols which are to be interpreted, not with language that is to be taken literally.

1. The measuring of the temple of God (1—2)

The apostle John is given 'a reed like a measuring rod' — a thick, heavy stick or something like that to measure size and dimensions. He is then directed to '**Go and measure the temple of God and the altar, and count the worshippers there.**'

But will you observe carefully that although the temple is the only area to be measured, it is not the only area that is mentioned? There are two other areas, though each is specifically excluded from the measuring – the outer court and the holy city. By the outer court is meant the open space which surrounds the temple itself but is nevertheless distinct from the temple, and by the holy city is meant earthly Jerusalem. Be sure that is clear in your mind. There are three areas. Starting with the largest, there is the holy city, then the outer court and then the temple itself. The court and the city are not to be measured. John is only to measure the temple, with its altar and worshippers.

What does this strange picture mean? We are being taught here concerning the nature of the true church of God. What is the true church of God? Of whom is it composed? Who belongs to it and who does not belong to it? What are its distinctive marks? What is its peculiar identity?

These are always matters of great importance, but especially so in our day with its crazy but very popular ecumenical thinking. There is terrible confusion over the very word 'church'. Some people continue to think that the word is limited to a building where services are held. Some people being ordained to the ministry speak of 'going into the church', which conjures up the picture of some sort of priestly class. Some people imagine that being a church member or belonging to a church consists of having undergone some rite or ceremony, like baptism or confirmation, or attending a place of worship either regularly or on the occasions when it suits them, like Christmas, Easter and Harvest. Some people assume that writing something like 'C. of E.' on their hospital admission forms does the job. But what 11:1 gives us is a set of three distinctive features or identity marks of the true church and its true members, which set them completely apart.

'Born of the Spirit'

'The temple' speaks symbolically of the new birth wrought by the Holy Spirit of God in the heart and life of everyone who becomes a Christian. Remember how Jesus insisted to Nicodemus: 'You must be born again' (John 3:7); 'I tell you the truth, no one can see [enter, ever belong to or become part of] the kingdom of God unless he is born again' (John 3:3). And recall, too, how on a number of

occasions in Scripture the word 'temple' is used to describe
the church ('a holy temple in the Lord . . . a dwelling in
which God lives by his Spirit', Ephesians 2:21—22) and
the Christian ('Don't you know that you yourselves are
God's temple and that God's Spirit lives in you? . . . God's
temple is sacred, and you are that temple' (1 Corinthians
3:16—17).

In a very special sense in the Old Testament God dwelt
in His temple. Now in a special sense He dwells in His
church — not in a bodily way but by His Holy Spirit. And so
the true church — that body, and that body alone, composed
of individually new-born souls — is His temple, His sanctuary
and His dwelling-place.

'Washed in his blood'

We know how full Revelation is of Old Testament allusions
and images. The Old Testament speaks so often of the altar
as the place of those sacrifices of God's appointment, commanded by Him and offered to Him by the priests on behalf
of the people. But all those altars and sacrifices and priests
pointed forward to one thing: Christ's sacrifice of Himself,
His shedding of His own blood for sinners at Calvary, as a
propitiatory sacrifice for our sins (that is, a sacrifice which
turned away God's wrath, satisfied God's justice, paid God's
penalty and, in all of this, demonstrated God's grace and
love). That is why Horatius Bonar could write:

> No blood, no altar now:
>   The sacrifice is o'er;
> No flame, no smoke ascends on high,
>   The lamb is slain no more.
> But richer blood has flowed from nobler veins,
> To purge the soul from guilt and cleanse the reddest
>   stains.

'Without the shedding of blood there is no forgiveness'
(Hebrews 9:22). And so the true church consists of those
who have had their sins washed clean through the blood of
Christ. Otherwise we could never have been reconciled to
God.

True worship

John was to 'measure the temple of God and the altar'.
He was also told to 'count the worshippers there'. Only
those who have been 'born of the Spirit, washed in His
blood' can bring true worship, acceptable worship, to God.
Only those who have been made worthy can set forth His
most worthy praise. The outward things of worship themselves (saying prayers, singing hymns and so on) are only
an empty shell and a mockery unless they proceed from
new-born, blood-washed hearts and souls.

But why the symbolism of the measuring? And what
of the outer court and the holy city? It adds up to a call to
examine our foundations. Paul urges, 'Examine yourselves
to see whether you are in the faith; test yourselves' (2 Corinthians 13:5), and that call could stand as a direct application
of the opening two verses of Revelation 11.

Not everything that has the name 'church' is in reality
the true church. Not when the three distinctive marks we
have just outlined are not visibly present. Hoeksema sums
it up very clearly like this: 'Three distinctions, therefore,
there were in Old Jerusalem: the city of Jerusalem proper,
the outer court, and finally the temple. So there were also
three distinctions in the spiritual Jerusalem of the New
Testament day: the Christian world, or the false church;
the show-church; and the true church of God, the spiritual
people of the Lord. It is to these that our text refers plainly.'

The holy city here, the city of Jerusalem as such, stands
for 'Christendom', the world of nominal Christianity, which
calls itself Christian and calls itself a church, which even
preaches maybe about the kingdom of God, but has no
hold upon the great truths of Christ and salvation, sin and
judgement, heaven and hell. The outer court (coming in a
little bit closer, you see) also pretends to be the true church,
but is hypocritical, worldly and represents the tares among
the wheat. 'They go with God's people to His temple for
worship, but they never enter the spiritual sanctuary of the
fellowship of God. They remain in the outer court.'[25]

Neither those in the holy city (the false church) nor the
outer court (the show church) are measured by John — that
is, they are not counted by God among His people, they
are not embraced under His peculiar sway and authority,

and so they do not enjoy His favour, security and protection. Rather have they 'been given to the Gentiles' who 'will trample' on them 'for 42 months'. By the Gentiles here are meant the pagans, the heathen, and the terrible truth is that all those who do not bear those distinctive marks of the true people of God, who do not belong to Him and worship Him in spirit and in truth, will gradually reveal themselves with increasing clarity and boldness as enemies of Christ and rejecters of the gospel. They will be seen to belong to the world's side, not the Lord's side. They will nail their colours to the mast of unbelief and fly the flag not of Christ but of Antichrist. Nominal Christendom and worldly Christianity will become the prey of every ungodly idea, whim and power. They will be trampled all over. Forty-two months is one of a number of symbolical descriptions of the gospel age (the period from the first coming – or the ascension – to the second coming of Christ).

Before we proceed any further, maybe everyone of us needs to spend some time, in the light of all this, meditating soberly upon Matthew 7:15–23.

2. The two witnesses (3–13)

The identity and security of the true church, the true people of God, has just been set before us in verses 1–2. The true church still remains in view in this central section of the chapter, but the emphasis falls now upon its witness and faithfulness.

The identity of the witnesses

Obviously the key to the right interpretation of these verses rests on the meaning of the 'two witnesses' (3). Many suggestions have been made as to who they are, including Moses and Elijah, Elijah and Elisha, Enoch and Elijah, the Law and the Prophets, the law and the gospel, the Old and New Testaments, and the Word and the Spirit! It is likely, however, that all those suggestions are too specific. We are on safer ground in following Hendriksen who says, 'The true church is now represented under the symbolism of two witnesses. These witnesses symbolize the church militant bearing testimony through its ministers and missionaries throughout the present dispensation.' And Wilson also is helpful: 'These witnesses are not actual men . . . They are rather a collective symbol of the church, for two witnesses were necessary to give competent legal testimony (Deuteronomy 17:6; 19:15).'

So what you have, in effect, in verses 3—13 is a panoramic view of church history throughout the gospel age. The '1,260 days' of verse 3 takes its place alongside the '42 months' of verse 2 and the 'time, times and half a time' of 12:14 as indicating that period. Wilson adds further, 'The purpose of the vision is to promote obedience: it is a summons to the church to bear witness to the truth before a hostile world.' It is the constant task of the church of Christ to witness to Him, to testify to the truth of the gospel and the claims of God, to make the Saviour known to needy and perishing sinners and to build up the righteous in the truth. All that is contained in **'they will prophesy'** (3), and the **'clothed in sackcloth'** is a reminder that the call to repentance is a fundamental thrust of that preaching, as well as an indication of the hard circumstances that will often be experienced in gospel work. Harking back to the end of chapter 10, we have here an illustration of the sweet and sour principle.

Our identifying of the two witnesses in this way is confirmed by the Zechariah 4 imagery to be found in verse 4. The two olive trees were probably representative of Zerubbabel the prince and Joshua the priest, 'the two who are anointed to serve the Lord of all the earth' (Zechariah 4:14), and symbolical of the people of God shining as lights in the world, while the lampstands stood for the oil of the Spirit, the mighty enabling and equipping power of God which ensures that the church's witness is not quenched. It must always be a case of ' "Not by might, nor by power, but by my Spirit," says the Lord Almighty' (Zechariah 4:6).

The power of the witnesses
The gospel is often thought of as a weak and weedy thing. Not so! Verses 5 and 6 picture its power, might and glory.

We know 'It is the power of God for the salvation of everyone who believes' (Romans 1:16). We have proved again and
again (and have learned from church history) that 'The
weapons we fight with . . . have divine power to demolish
strongholds . . . demolish arguments and every pretension
that sets itself up against the knowledge of God . . . take
captive every thought to make it obedient to Christ' (2 Corinthians 10:4–5). And the destructive power of the gospel is
especially in view here (5). Those who would set themselves
up as destroyers of the gospel will end up themselves being
destroyed by the gospel. While to those who believe, Christ
is precious, yet to those who do not believe He is 'a stone
that causes men to stumble and a rock that makes them fall'
(Isaiah 8:14 quoted in 1 Peter 2:8).

The ministries of Elijah and Moses are recalled in verses
5–6 by way of example: Elijah calling down fire from
heaven to consume the soldiers who sought to arrest him
(2 Kings 1) and praying that it would not rain (1 Kings
17; cf. James 5:16–17), and Moses turning the waters of
the Nile into blood and smiting Egypt with numerous
plagues (Exodus 7–11).

The gospel is not impotent! The gospel will not fail!
Rather the question prompted by all this should be 'How
shall we escape if we ignore such a great salvation?'
(Hebrews 2:3.) The church of God will share in judging
the world.

The killing of the witnesses
The history of the progress of the gospel is an up-and-down
one. That is to say, there are periods of apparent blessing
and periods of seeming defeat, seasons of refreshing and
seasons of retreat, times when everything throbs with life
and power, with people crying out, 'What must I do to be
saved?' and thousands pressing into the kingdom, and times
when there seems no response, when everything seems
barren and discouraging, hard as flint.

In Amos 8:9–12 the prophet used a striking phrase:
'a famine of hearing the words of the Lord'; one such famine
time is pictured symbolically in verses 7–10 of Revelation 11.

We have seen something already (and chapters 12 and 13
will teach us much more) of Christ and the church's great

enemy, Satan, whose abode is the very pit of hell. While he
is active all the time, there are days when Satan's onslaught
is particularly furious and (it seems) his success is on a
grand scale. Here we can see him 'triumphing' over the
witnesses, whose dead bodies lie open to gaze and ridicule
'in the street of the great city, which is figuratively called
Sodom and Egypt, where also their Lord was crucified'.

Sodom and Egypt stand in turn for uncleanness and the
cruel oppression of God's people. 'The great city' is
Jerusalem, whose inhabitants crucified the Saviour. 'Because
of its immorality and persecution of the saints it has become
spiritually like Sodom and Egypt,' observes Dr Hendriksen.
It thinks it has killed the church, put out its light, quenched
its witness. And so there is great rejoicing – everyone has
a party and gives each other presents, thinking that at last
their tormentors have been destroyed. How the world loves
a dead church! Such a church is always a favourite with
those who reject Christ (even if, remembering verses 1–2,
they might occupy positions in the outer court or the city
itself). Outward forms in which there is no spiritual life –
patterns and programmes in which Christ takes no place –
all this suits the devil and the world down to the ground!
Just think how many rejoiced to see Christ crucified –
and even Herod and Pilate became friends!

But notice that all this lasts only for 'three and a half
days' (9) – in other words, the apparent triumphs of the
godless are very, very brief and ultimately, of course, they
are no triumphs at all!

The revival of the witnesses
Can you imagine the shock-waves that would go through
you if a dead body you had been staring at suddenly got
up? That's exactly what is recorded in verses 11–13!
'A breath of life from God entered them, and they stood
on their feet, and terror struck those who saw them' (11).
Wilson's telling comment is 'The world has often celebrated
the death of the church, only to see it rise again from the
verge of extinction.'

It happened in the days of the Reformation after all the
grim days of medieval darkness and Romanism. It happened
in the days of the Puritans in England during the seventeenth

century and at the Kirk o'Shotts in Scotland under John
Livingstone's preaching in 1630. It happened again in the
eighteenth century when God used men like Jonathan
Edwards in North America, Whitefield and Wesley in England
and Rowland and Harris in Wales. It happened during the
ministry of John Elias in Anglesey at the beginning of the
nineteenth century, when forty-four chapels were built on
that island in forty years. It has happened again and again
and again – for God is the living God, the gospel is the
living gospel and the church is the church of the living God
and made up of living stones. Just at the very moment when
the world thinks it has won a glorious victory, the tables
are turned.

And so it will always be, right through to the final 'Come
up here' (12). Stop and read through Matthew 24:9–14,
to take in the Saviour's own words on these matters. When
the end eventually comes and all is being got ready for the
judgement at Christ's glorious return, how the world will
be paralysed with fear as they behold, too late, the reality
of God, the truth of the gospel and the glory of the church!
No secret rapture this, but God acknowledging His servants
before their enemies – then judging and destroying those
enemies and casting them out of His presence for ever!
Their giving Him glory (13) is not upon their conversion;
rather is it a recognition by them at last of His sovereignty
and power, but at a time when they will be receiving the
sharp end of it. For the day of repentance and grace will
be over. All is ready for the final judgement. The world
remains as unrepentant as ever.

Do not be ashamed of the gospel!
Do not underestimate the power of the gospel!
Do not despair that revival will never come!
Do not neglect the application of the gospel to your own
  soul!

3. The blowing of the seventh trumpet (14–19)

It seems a long time since the sixth trumpet was blown!
In fact it was back in 9:13. The final trumpet is also

described as the third woe (14), yet it is striking that rather than being just a description of judgement, the material of this final section of Revelation 11 is also something of a beyond-the-judgement peep at the glorious kingdom of Christ. The great keynote of the section is found in verse 15: **'The kingdom of the world has become the kingdom of our Lord and of his Christ, and he will reign for ever and ever.'** Wonderful!

Victory for Christ

All through the Bible, let alone in the book of Revelation, the certain goal is held out of Christ being victorious over all His enemies. Think of how the apostle Paul expresses it when he looks forward confidently to the time when 'at the name of Jesus every knee should bow, in heaven and on earth and under the earth, and every tongue confess that Jesus Christ is Lord, to the glory of God the Father' (Philippians 2:10–11). Well, here we are at last! The kingdom, the power and the glory are Christ's, and Christ's alone.

As the seventh angel sounded his trumpet, loud voices sang together in heaven the magnificent song of verse 15. It seems as if all heaven has been on tenterhooks, on the edge of its seat, waiting for the final accomplishment of all God's plans.

Notice the singular **'kingdom of the world'**, not the plural 'kingdoms'. Why is that? Surely the world is composed of many separate kingdoms. In a national sense that is quite true. But the point here is that Christ rules as the sole and unopposed King over the whole world, because the one to whom dominion once seemed to belong (Satan) has now had to give it up. It is a picture of the undisputed sovereignty of the Lord Jesus Christ – indeed we could translate it: 'The sovereignty of the world has become the sovereignty of our Lord . . .'

You remember how during the Falklands War, in the early 1980s, 'sovereignty' was a word in constant use? Britain claimed sovereignty of the islands. So did Argentina. The matter was in dispute. But the sovereignty of the world (15) is not in dispute – there are no rival claims that can stand. Christ is all and is over all and is in all. How wonderful it will be to see all opposition to Christ finally abolished!

Of course, He reigns already now. But He is not at present unopposed. But the blowing of the seventh trumpet will be the cue for the song: 'The Lord reigns!' And, what is more, **'He will reign for ever and ever.'**

It was made plain way back in Daniel 7:14 that 'His dominion is an everlasting dominion that will not pass away, and his kingdom is one that will never be destroyed.' And the announcement of His coming birth involved the declaration from the angel that 'His kingdom will never end' (Luke 1:33).

Fulness of joy for God's people

Just look at the reaction of the twenty-four elders in verse 16 to the news of verse 15. They got down from their thrones, **'fell on their faces and worshipped God'.** Rightly so! What other reaction could possibly be appropriate?

Much earlier in our exposition I interpreted the twenty-four elders as representative of the completeness of the Old Testament and New Testament church of Christ, and I still hold to that interpretation here. They knew God was sovereign. That is a point that every believer knows – God is sovereign in creation, in His election of grace, His providence, His administration – indeed in everything. If you do not believe that, then it must be that you are not content to take the word of Scripture and believe it. And if you are not content to do that, then your whole profession of Christ is open to serious question. Yet although we know this truth of God's sovereignty now, the final revelation of it will bring an unspeakable joy and delight to those who love the Saviour.

It will mean fulness of joy, because He has finally and fully and visibly taken His great power and begun to reign (17). By the way, if you compare 11:17 with 1:8, what is the difference? It is this: 1:8 speaks of the Lord God Almighty 'who is, and who was, and who is to come', while 11:17 omits the 'who is to come'. This is not because His eternity is suddenly in doubt, but because He now has come and declared Himself most decisively!

It will mean fulness of joy, secondly, because this day of victory for Christ is also the day for rewarding His servants (18). God loves to reward His children, though all His rewards, it must be remembered, are rewards of His grace and never of our earning or achievement. The prophets will be rewarded. All the saints of God who revere His name will be rewarded and 'both small and great' (famous and obscure, bright lights and lesser lights, heroes of faith and those whose faith was like a grain of mustard seed, those whose ministries were blessed to the saving of multitudes, along with every faithful and approved gospel minister, however much he was opposed, and so on). Not just the greats of evangelical church history, but the 'common people' among God's flock, the silent and unthanked labourers, the unknown servants of God who plodded on faithfully, the weak and timid ones, the children who loved their Redeemer and their teachers who taught them of Him, the godly parents who sought amidst much trial and heartache and disappointment to train up their children in the way of the Lord and to honour God in their families . . . Not one missing. Not one forgotten.

Fearful judgement for God's enemies
There has to be this side to the picture as well. The wrath of God must be faced if the grace of God has been refused. There are no other alternatives. For the great day to which everything is leading up — just as the ticking of the clock must inevitably lead to the exploding of the device to which it is connected — will bring misery and ruin to all those who have passed God by, do not love Him and have not feared His holy name. It will be a day 'for destroying those who destroy the earth' (18).

The chapter ends in verse 19 with the opening of God's temple in heaven and the revealing of the ark of the covenant. Even this confirms the double aspect of grace and wrath. The ark of the covenant speaks to the believer of God's covenant of grace, of His mercy to sinners, of fellowship with God and His presence with His people. It is most blessed and cheering. It assures us that all God's purposes for us are now fulfilled. But that opening of the heavenly temple and manifesting of the ark is accompanied also by solemn reminders of God's majesty and power: 'flashes of lightning, rumblings, peals of thunder, an earthquake and a great hailstorm'. God is God!

12.
Satan at work

Please read Revelation 12

The book of Revelation has already had plenty to say about the conflict between the church and the world. We saw repeatedly in the letters to the seven churches how great and persistent are the pressures upon Christian men and women to conform to the world, and that the penalty for refusal to conform is often abuse or persecution from the world, leading sometimes even to the loss of your job, the assassination of your character and ultimately for some even imprisonment and death. It is never easy to be a Christian. There is this constant struggle going on between the church and the world, between the Christian and society. We are aware of it first of all from Scripture itself. But we see it also from a consideration of history, and what is more we feel and experience it in our own Christian life and witness. The Lord Jesus Christ Himself has warned us, 'If the world hates you, keep in mind that it hated me first' (John 15:18).

What we find to be the great concern of the second part of the book, however, now that we have reached the half-way point, is to demonstrate that this church-world struggle is but the outward manifestation of the behind-the-scenes conflict being fought between the Lord Jesus Christ and Satan. This war being waged in time and history has a cosmic dimension and this the apostle Paul speaks of when he insists, 'Our struggle is not against flesh and blood, but against the rulers, against the authorities, against the powers of this dark world and against the spiritual forces of evil in the heavenly realms' (Ephesians 6:12). Chapters 12 and 13 open up the account of this matter, with their focus upon the character and opposition of the enemies of God. First of all we meet Satan at work (chapter 12) and then we are introduced to Satan's right-hand men (chapter 13).

Chapter 12 falls into three scenes which we shall map out straight away as a guide to the territory we are about to investigate:

1. Satan purposing to destroy Christ (1–12).
2. Satan, having failed in that design, turns his attention to destroying the church of Christ (13–16).
3. Satan's work against the individual Christians who make up Christ's church (17).

Satan versus Christ

The chapter opens with John's observation that '**A great and wondrous sign appeared in heaven.**' And what a strange sign or symbol it turned out to be! Without failing to see the wood for the trees (remember it is through their insistence on finding an interpretation for every last and tiniest detail that so many interpreters of Revelation have gone wrong), we can identify three main characters. In order of appearance they are '**a woman clothed with the sun**' (1), '**an enormous red dragon**' (3) and '**the male child of the woman to whom she gave birth**' (4–5). What are we to make of these characters?

Consider the woman first of all. By this sign we are to understand the church of God, the people of God in both Old and New Testament days. The details ('**clothed with the sun, with the moon under her feet and a crown of twelve stars on her head**') speak together of the radiance and glory of God's church, which later on in the book is described beautifully as Christ's bride.

Now we have to admit that, as we look around, the thought of the church being glorious may seem rather far-fetched and hard to believe. The church on earth at the present time, generally speaking, seems to be very far from glorious. Worldliness, materialism, small numbers, false doctrine, spiritual sluggishness and carelessness seem to abound on every side and in the view of many the church has become a laughing-stock with nothing to say that is

worth hearing and nothing to contribute of any real value.
They regard it as redundant. The church often looks like a
'has-been' or an 'also-ran'.

But things are very different from the viewpoint of
heaven! From that aspect the church is all-glorious! The
psalmist declares, 'Glorious things are said of you, O city
of God' (Psalm 87:3). And chapters like Isaiah 60 and 62
are wonderfully full of the same theme: 'The Lord rises
upon you and his glory appears over you' (Isaiah 60:2).
'You will be a crown of splendour in the Lord's hand, a
royal diadem in the hand of your God' (Isaiah 62:3). And
the names Hephzibah (speaking of God's delight in His
church) and Beulah (God's marriage to His church) are
mentioned in that same chapter and give a mouth-watering
taste of the glory of the church!

The thing to grasp is this: it is not only that the church
will be glorious, or that in seasons of revival the church is
glorious. More than that — the church is essentially glorious;
glorious, that is, in its very essence and nature as the elect
people of God, the purchased possession of the Saviour and
the dwelling-place of God by His Holy Spirit!

The woman is described as 'pregnant' and 'about to give
birth' (2), and then we are told that 'She gave birth to a
son, a male child' (5). The child in the sign must be the
Lord Jesus Christ, the one spoken of way back in the first
messianic prophecy of Scripture (Genesis 3:15) as the seed
or offspring of the woman who would crush the serpent's
head. This interpretation is confirmed by the statement in
verse 5 with respect to His character and work, ruling all the
nations with an iron sceptre. That has clear shades of Psalm
2:7–9 and we have already come across it in the promise
attached to the letter to Thyatira (2:27).

But, you may ask, how is the church (the woman) to be
understood as giving birth to Christ (the male child)? Surely
that does not make sense. Yes it does! We must remember
two things. The first is the licence that must be allowed
in visionary and symbolic picture writing. Such language
cannot always be pinned down too neatly or too tightly,
for the very reason that it is symbolic and not literal. But
the second thing is this. While we know that the Lord Jesus
Christ is God and that voluntarily, and in complete obedience

to the Father's will, He left the glory of heaven for a season and 'made himself nothing, taking the very nature of a servant, being made in human likeness' (Philippians 2:7), yet gloriously and miraculously, He is also represented in Scripture from the human side as coming from an earthly line. Romans 9:5 sets this forth very clearly: 'From them [the patriarchs] is traced the human ancestry of Christ, who is God over all, for ever praised!' So too do verses like Isaiah 11:1 and Romans 1:3, along with many others.

As for the dragon — there are no prizes for guessing whom he represents! He is clearly identified in verse 9 by some of his names and aliases: '**that ancient serpent called the devil or Satan, who leads the whole world astray**'. His seven heads indicate his power and knowledge. His ten horns speak of his power to destroy. His seven crowns testify to his thirst for authority and his imagination that he possesses it. The apostle Paul describes him as '**the god of this age**' (2 Corinthians 4:4). The reference to the stars (4) ties in with 2 Peter 2:4 and Jude 6 once more and speaks of the evil spirits (fallen angels) whom Satan took with him when he fell from heaven.

Satan's intention is immediately exposed in verse 4 — he aims to destroy Christ! '**Devour**' is a chilling verb. He had been conspicuously unsuccessful in this work during the Old Testament period. Although he had seen to it that godly Abel was slain by his brother Cain, yet he had not bargained for Seth being born to Adam and Eve and the godly line of the Messiah coming through Seth. The universal destruction at the time of the flood did not enable him to get his way either, for righteous Noah was preserved and once again the godly line was secured. It looked as if his big break was going to come with the slaying of Isaac, Abraham's son through whom the covenant promises were to be fulfilled, but we know the blessed outcome of that episode! Then instead of being wiped out in Egypt, the people of God were brought forth by God's mighty hand and outstretched arm — what a magnificent phrase that is! And you can go on tracing this same theme of Satan's bold attempts and utter failures right the way through the Old Testament.[26]

Then when Jesus was born Satan sought to work through

Herod, who desired to kill the young child and sought to elicit information from the wise men which would enable him to do so. But all to no avail. He was completely foiled! The Lord Jesus Christ went on to Calvary to die for sinners. He rose again, leading captivity captive, destroying death and opening up for us the gate of eternal life. And He '**was snatched up to God and to his throne**' (5), which is a symbolic reference to His ascension, which removed Christ once and for all out of the devil's evil reach.

Just a word on verses 7–9. 'There was war in heaven.' Imagine that as the main headline on the news! Michael is mentioned. He and his angels were on one side in this war and the dragon and his angels were on the other side, and the whole confrontation issued in Satan being hurled out of heaven and down to earth. This is a vivid symbolical way of emphasizing Satan's utter inability to destroy Christ, and, by implication, his inability to destroy those for whom Christ died. By the way, Michael appears in the Old Testament in Daniel 10 and 12 as the chief and great prince and in the New Testament in Jude 9 as the archangel. He stands here, says Dr Hendriksen, as 'leader of the good angels and defender of God's people'.

Not surprisingly this victory over Satan is greeted with joyful songs in heaven (10–11). Yet despite what is stated unequivocally concerning Christ's victory and Satan's discomfiting, that does not mean that the devil just walks away quietly, accepting his defeat like a gentleman. Satan is no gentleman! Which leads us, via verse 12, to the next section of the chapter.

Satan versus the church

Although God's kingdom and Christ's authority are assured and firm, although none of the Evil One's attempts to accuse or destroy the brethren can ultimately get anywhere (for who is to condemn those for whom Christ has died and whom God has justified?) and although death for Christ is gain and cannot harm us, yet 'Watch out, church!' is the keynote of verses 13–16.

Verse 12 is the bridge passage. Heaven can rejoice, but

'Woe to the earth and the sea, because the devil has gone down to you!' Utterly frustrated in his attempts to destroy Christ, Satan's great aim now is to pursue the church (the woman) instead. He is doomed to failure. His time of activity is limited. Yet this only inflames his fury and antagonism. But the loveliest thing is this: the church of God is safe. 'As the mountains surround Jerusalem, so the Lord surrounds his people, both now and for evermore' (Psalm 125:2). The wings of the eagle, the place prepared in the desert, the earth opening its mouth to swallow the river that had flowed out of the dragon's mouth — all these symbolic details underscore the security of the church of Christ. The word rendered 'taken care of' (14) or 'nourished' (AV) is used of feeding and nursing the young of animals. The church will be kept alive! And this is so throughout the whole of the gospel era ('a time, times and half a time', 14).

There will be, and we know that there is, harsh persecution of the church, for some regimes are committed to the complete extermination of Christianity. There will be the devil's attempts to conform the church to the world — the line that any religion will do, that treasures on earth really do pay, that the church should be in the state's pocket, that sexual deviations condemned by God are deviations no longer, and so on. He has all manner of tricks, wiles, devices and schemes (Ephesians 6:11) to get us to water down the gospel in order to make it more 'palatable' to sinners. One contemporary minister, Dr Robert Schuller, famous for his Crystal Cathedral, is reported as writing, 'I have no right to offend the self-esteem of a person under the motivation or guise of saving his soul,' and 'Don't tell them they're sinners. They'll believe you — and you'll reinforce this self-image.'[27]

The devil will seek to hinder the church's usefulness and make her lose her saltiness. He will seek to disturb local congregations, so that they end up 'biting and devouring each other' and being 'destroyed by each other' (Galatians 5:15). 'Ichabod' ('the Glory has departed') will be written over some churches as God departs from them and they fall into ruins or are sold to be warehouses or mosques.

But although Satan will appear to be having great success, remember that the true church of Jesus Christ is indestructible. Has He not said, 'I will build my church, and the gates of hell will not overcome it'? (Matthew 16: 18.) Has He not 'loved the church and [given] himself up for her to make her holy, cleansing her by the washing with water through the word, and to present her to himself as a radiant church, without stain or wrinkle or any other blemish, but holy and blameless'? (Ephesians 5:25–27.)

Satan versus individual Christians

In the last verse of the chapter (17) the whole work of Satan is particularized. Each individual Christian is a marked target for the devil's attacks — a fact of which the apostle John, in exile on the island of Patmos, was only too well aware! He 'went off to make war against the rest of her offspring'. Just notice in passing from this verse the description of a Christian that it provides, with the emphasis upon our obedience to God's commandments and our faithful adherence to the gospel testimony.

The fact that we have a great and powerful enemy of our souls is an abiding theme in Scripture. Peter expresses it very vividly when he writes, 'Be self-controlled and alert. Your enemy the devil prowls around like a roaring lion looking for someone to devour' (1 Peter 5:8). If you have ever visited a safari park (or actually been on safari in Africa!) you will soon get the picture of a hungry lion waiting to pounce upon its food, tear it apart and devour it! And in this connection the names of Satan, some of which have already been mentioned in this chapter, are important. Names in Scripture are not only handles for identification; they indicate characters and ways. Here are some of his: 'Satan', which means adversary or false accuser; 'dragon', picturing a strong and frightening monster; 'serpent', reminding us how cunning and deceitful he is; 'devil', which means slanderer. There is nothing nice or truthful about him!

Back in 1652 the Puritan minister Thomas Brooks wrote a treatise called *Precious Remedies against Satan's Devices,* which has recently been republished.[28] Even the contents pages make searching and profitable reading. Very comprehensively he details 38 devices and 196 remedies (if I added

them up correctly!). But how vital it is that we take them
seriously, for knowing your enemy is half the battle! Here
are just a few areas of the devil's activity that we must be
ready to deal with.

1. He will seek to draw us back into sin, especially into
those particular sins which figured largely in our pre-
conversion life.

2. He will try to overwhelm us with a view of our past
and present sins, suggesting that they are not wiped out or
are too large or too repeated for God to deal with them.

3. He will remind us of our frequent relapses into sins
formerly repented of and prayed against, implying that we are
not making any progress or headway in the Christian life.

4. He loves to persuade Christians that repentance is an
easy matter that we can just take in our stride, so we need
not have any second thoughts or scruples about sinning
against God — no mention from Satan of the misery of sin, the
forlornness of having God hide His face from us, the agony of
repentance or the nature of true godly sorrow for sin.

5. He seeks to persuade us that all that glitters in the world
that we have forsaken is gold after all.

6. He does all that he can to remove our assurance of
salvation — sometimes by making us think that our salvation
itself and our continuance in it depends upon us, sometimes
by twisting our view of God's love and fatherly care towards
us when we face discouragements and afflictions, sometimes
by suggesting that the promises of God's Word are in-
sufficient to meet our needs and case.

7. And he will draw our attention to the supposed happiness
and freedom enjoyed by those who are walking in the paths
of sin, over and against the crosses, losses, sufferings and
sorrows that daily attend those who seek self-denyingly
after Christ and holiness.

'Resist him, standing firm in the faith' (1 Peter 5:9).
Remember this: He who is for us and within us is far, far
greater than he who is against us. So Charles Wesley can
write, and we can sing:

> Jesus! the name high over all,
> In hell, or earth, or sky;
> Angels and men before it fall,
> And devils fear and fly.

13.
Satan's right-hand men

Please read Revelation 13

These two chapters, 12 and 13, belong very closely together,
setting forth so clearly the character and opposition of the
enemies of God. Chapter 12 has been full of what Satan
seeks to do; now chapter 13 gives us a view of other branches
of his work and introduces us to his right-hand helpers or
henchmen, who turn out to be two of the nastiest bits of
work to be found in the Bible. We must remember that
John's symbolic vision continues without a break.

As John looked, the dragon himself 'stood on the shore
of the sea' (1), and then the two monster-like beasts
appeared, like something from a horror film. One arose
out of the sea (1) and one out of the earth (11). Stating
our conclusions first, and then tracing the details that bring
us to these conclusions, we may say that the first beast
represents Satan's persecuting power via world authorities,
and the second beast represents his perverting of Christianity.
It goes without saying that these two beasts, these agents
of Satan, work in the very closest co-operation; indeed
they are invariably hand-in-glove.

The beast out of the sea

This character who appears in verses 1—10, then, stands for
Satan's persecuting power which is constantly at work in
history through governments, rulers, totalitarian states,
dictators and atheistic regimes of one kind or another.
This is borne out by the main details of John's vision.

The beast had 'ten horns and seven heads, with ten crowns

on his horns'. These stand for his boastful self-importance, his deceived imagining of having great dominion, yet none-theless his very real power. Never underestimate the devil's power. One of his most successful con-tricks, remember, is to get people to think that he does not really exist, or that he is just some harmless cartoon figure with horns and a pointed tail to be joked about.

This interpretation is further confirmed with the description given in verse 2 of his leopard-bear-lion looks. Those who are familiar with Daniel 7 will hear bells ringing — the similarly described beasts mentioned there represent successive world empires that came and went.

Then notice the way both the dragon and the beast take to themselves the prerogative of worship which belongs only to God (1, 4—6). The blasphemous names on each of the beast's heads and its express hatred of God and every-thing to do with God are familiar features of his character. They were demonstrated in first-century emperor worship, which we already know was such a problem for those Christians to whom the book of Revelation was addressed initially, and who faced the choice of affirming 'Jesus is Lord!' and being sent to prison or put to death, or of bowing down to the state with a cry of 'Caesar is Lord!'. They have been repeated down the ages of history and are still manifested in those contemporary regimes who insist upon the supremacy of the state and the registration of 'official' churches. And, sad to say, the reaction of astonishment and blind allegiance from the world (3—4) does not change either. People are so gullible, so easily led, so readily sucked into the system.

The mention of the fatal wound which had been healed (3) makes the point further that, while particular govern-ments and enemies of true Christianity will come and go, rise and fall, the underlying principle of Christ versus Satan, worldly authority versus Christ's authority, the true church versus the state, continues all the time throughout the gospel age ('forty-two months', 5). In John's own lifetime Nero may have gone, but Domitian had come. There was no respite, nor will there be until the Lord Jesus Christ comes again in glory to judge and condemn His enemies and to gather together His elect.

The call to 'patient endurance and faithfulness' (10) arises naturally, lest our hearts begin to fail us for fear. The picture of the beast's power and apparent success in verses 7–8 is quite terrifying. But look what else is mentioned there: 'the book of life belonging to the Lamb that was slain from the creation of the world' (8). 'Therefore, there is now no condemnation for those who are in Christ Jesus' (Romans 8:1). The constant security of every believer in the Lord Jesus Christ is a glorious reality. Nothing can ever change our election from eternity! Right now, just stop and linger for a moment over John 10:27–30. Wonderful words!

All this may seem a long way off from the difficulties even of being a Christian in the United Kingdom. But we must not take our civil and religious liberties for granted. At the moment we may meet freely, worship freely, distribute the Scriptures freely and evangelize freely. But governments are fickle and the power of the beast out of the sea is great. We must work while it is day, not sit about and rest. The tide may turn even for us, just as it has already turned for so many of our Christian brethren in other lands. As I write this, Sunday is facing increasing attack from those who want to remove all trading restraints, and so on. It is not being melodramatic or over-reacting to suggest that that could turn into the sphere where religious persecution in this country begins.

But whatever happens, do not fear! They may even kill our bodies, but they cannot have our souls! What magnificent consolation this must have brought to the tried and persecuted believers in John's day — but is it not precious to us also?

The beast out of the earth

This character who appears in verses 11–18 is as ugly as his friend and stands for Satan's perverting of Christianity. This is one of his regular arenas of activity.

Look straight away at verse 11: 'He had two horns like a lamb, but he spoke like a dragon.' That gives him away! What could be more harmless or attractive than a lamb, especially a new-born one skipping about in the meadow or feeding from a bottle held in a child's hand? But this beast is no little lamb! Pretending to be one thing but in reality being something very different is one of Satan's cleverest and most-practised tricks. He is the great impersonator, the master of disguises. Paul draws attention to this in a portion of one of his epistles where he has been speaking of false teachers. He writes, 'For such men are false apostles, deceitful workmen, masquerading as apostles of Christ. And no wonder, for Satan himself masquerades as an angel of light. It is not surprising, then, if his servants masquerade as servants of righteousness.' And then he adds, 'Their end will be what their actions deserve' (2 Corinthians 11:13—15). The Lord Jesus Christ Himself describes the devil as 'a liar and the father of lies' (John 8:44), while 19:20 of Revelation speaks of this beast as 'the false prophet'. Be warned!

As you read through the verses of this section you cannot help but be struck by the subtlety and success of the devil both now and in the past. There is his constant desire to copy and counterfeit everything that God does (13), so that many are taken in and overwhelmed. 'For false Christs and false prophets will appear and perform great signs and miracles to deceive even the elect — if that were possible' (Matthew 24:24). He brings counterfeit preaching, counterfeit conversions, counterfeit miracles, counterfeit healings, counterfeit experiences. In fact, you name it and the beast out of the earth counterfeits it! Here are all the false religions and cults, all the '-ologies' and '-isms' which have littered the generations. So many of them appear at first glance to have a superficial veneer of Christianity about them, but upon closer investigation are found to be striking at the very root and heart of the true gospel of the Lord Jesus Christ. Especially is this true with respect to the doctrine of the person and work of Christ Himself and we are reminded of John Newton's lines which are very appropriate:

'What think ye of Christ?' is the test
To try both your state and your scheme;
You cannot be right in the rest,
Until you think rightly of Him.

Think of the Jehovah's Witnesses, who come knocking on our doors and open up the conversation with such a harmless-sounding: 'Good afternoon, we are Bible students,' yet their view of Christ dethrones Him from the Godhead, not to mention their many errors in other areas of doctrine. Or think of the Mormons, with their deceptively courteous manner and earnest attitude, but to them the Lord Jesus Christ is a 'god amongst the council of the gods' — outright blasphemy!

Then there are the Christian Scientists, with their churches and reading rooms all over the place, and their view of Christ which distinguishes between 'Jesus the human man and Christ the divine idea', and their depersonalizing of God into 'good'. Or, again, the Spiritualists, who have the nerve to call themselves a church, yet are steeped in evil and blaspheme the Saviour by calling Him 'a medium of a very high order'. What a synagogue of Satan they are!

And the beast out of the earth has many other deceptive guises as well. There is the Unification Church (Moonies), with their hold upon people. There is the whole business of sending money off to some agency in return for promised prayer and healing that has folk getting out their cheque books without a second thought. And we must include Freemasonry as well, for that belongs right in the pit, with its blasphemous oaths over an open Bible and its code of secrecy. The fact that bishops, high-up men in the armed forces, medical men, men in business, law and banking, government men and so on belong is not to weigh anything with us at all. 'What harmony is there between Christ and Belial [the devil]?' (2 Corinthians 6:15). The clear call to the Christian with regard to Freemasonry is 'Come out from them and be separate' (2 Corinthians 6:17), and the same goes for all the other things we have mentioned.

And ultimately we have to put Roman Catholicism among these delusions worked by the beast out of the earth as well. For that whole system utterly deceives men and women into thinking they are right with God on their own merits or with the help of Mary, saints or priests, while it denies the cardinal truth of justification by God's grace alone and through faith in Christ alone as the only way of receiving salvation, righteousness and heaven.

What is the meaning of verses 16—17? It is 'a parody of the sealing of the redeemed (7:3)' is Wilson's excellent comment. Remember that the sealing there stood for God's ownership of His people. Here it stands for the mark of the beast's ownership; it is no more an actual visible mark of branding than was the seal of chapter 7, but it declares the terrible truth that those who worship the beast, those who oppose Christ, are branded as belonging to the kingdom of darkness and so partake of the evil character (and will one day partake of the everlasting punishment) of the one to whom they belong. Notice that the mark is on their right hand and their forehead. 'The forehead symbolizes the mind, the thought-life, the philosophy of a person. The right hand indicates his deed, action, trade, industry,' remarks Hendriksen. In other words, a person's Christ-rejecting spirit is very evident in all he thinks, says and does, and in how he lives and the priorities he follows. As for verse 17, remember how already the Christians in Smyrna were feeling the pinch of economic sanctions because they insisted upon remaining true to Christ (2:9).

A final word: what do we make of verse 18 and the famous 'number of the beast', 666? There has been any amount of fanciful speculation about this, even with novels being written and films being made! Yet at the risk of appearing simplistic or a know-all, surely the matter is quite clear when we take it not in limbo but against the background of all that we have learned so far from the book of Revelation.

We have observed the importance of numbers, and that one of the most frequent numbers is seven — seven spirits, seven churches, seven seals, seven trumpets, seven bowls. Seven stands for perfection (the seven spirits of God speaking of the divine glory and perfection of the Holy Spirit of God) and completeness (the churches not being the only seven that existed, but representing Christ's church and its conditions at all times). Surely, then, six stands for imperfection and incompleteness — nearly seven, but not quite. So near and yet so far! So 777 would stand for supreme perfection (if there could be such a thing!) and 666 stands for persistent failure, repeated frustration, permanently missing the mark. That is why it is called 'man's number'.

Do you see the point that is being taught? Whatever the power at present in control — atheistic or communist regimes, cold and calculating governments, lawless trade unions, and all the beast's conning counterfeits of true religion — they fall short, they are doomed, they cannot win.

When we come to chapters 19 and 20 we shall find in detail the fall and destruction of Satan, the beast and the false prophet. In contrast, hear Jesus' words about Himself: 'All authority in heaven and on earth has been given to me' (Matthew 28:18). At His name alone shall every knee bow! To Him alone will the glorious title Lord be ascribed!

Let Martin Luther have the last word for now:

> And were this world all devils o'er,
>   And watching to devour us,
> We lay it not to heart so sore;
>   Not they can overpower us.
>   And let the prince of ill
>   Look grim as e'er he will,
>   He harms us not a whit;
>   For why? his doom is writ;
> A word shall quickly slay him.

14.
Triumph or reckoning?

Please read Revelation 14

These are days when people do not like things to be too 'black and white'. They have no taste for talk that is too dogmatic. 'Unbending, hard-line, uncompromising' are charges that are frequently levelled. This is true widely and generally, but it is especially true in matters of religion. And so we have the rise of the ecumenical movement, the World Council of Churches, the British Council of Churches, multi-faith services, and who knows what else — all searching for supposed 'grey areas' where people can sink their differences and abandon their distinctives; 'grey areas' where as many people as possible can pitch their tents and be happy, even though in reality their convictions and practices may be poles apart.

Revelation 14 is no 'grey area'! It is bracketed around, at its beginning and its close, with two of the most important and practical realities that we can ever consider: heaven and hell. The chapter divides quite clearly into three parts:
1. The Lamb with His people (1—5).
2. The angels with their message (6—13).
3. The harvest with its judgements (14—20).

The Lamb with His people

After the grimness and horror of the two preceding chapters, we may feel greatly relieved and overjoyed to come now and breathe a very different air that is clear and pure, in verses 1—5. These verses are not hard to interpret. They present the twin and glorious realities of the victory of the Lord

Jesus Christ over all His enemies and the security of all those who belong to Him — themes that have already been expounded in some measure in the book.

When John looked, the first person to occupy his gaze was 'the Lamb'. The Lamb, without any argument, is the Lord Jesus Christ. We may be sure of that! He was '**standing on Mount Zion**'.

This chapter is just as much a symbolic picture as the ones that have gone before and so we are not to understand the literal mountain in Jerusalem, but heaven itself — that 'Mount Zion, which cannot be shaken, but endures for ever' (Psalm 125:1); that 'heavenly Jerusalem, the city of the living God' (Hebrews 12:22). And who are there with Christ? The 144,000 — remember them? We met them back in chapter 7:4, where we identified them with the company of chapter 7:9 — the whole elect of God. This is confirmed by the fact of their having Christ's name and the Father's name written on their foreheads. Of whom could that be true, except of the redeemed? Christ's people belong to Him. They are all there. Not one is missing, just as Christ promised (John 6:39).

> The Lamb with His fair army
> Doth on Mount Zion stand,
> And glory, glory dwelleth
> In Immanuel's land
>   (Anne Ross Cousin).

As in the vision of heaven in chapters 4 and 5, the sight John saw was accompanied by the song he heard. He heard a most amazing sound coming out of heaven. It was all at once like '**the roar of rushing waters . . . a loud peal of thunder . . . harpists playing their harps**'. It was strong, thunderous and majestic, yet it was also sensitive, tender and sweet. In a real sense it defied description in words — better listened to than written about!

What was happening was that the whole symbolic 144,000 were in full voice together singing '**a new song**' of praise to God. As we observed earlier in our study, only those who have a new heart can sing a new song. The praises of Jesus are the preserve of Christians only.

Some commentators have seen all sorts of problems surrounding verses 4–5, but again the meaning is not hard to find. One of the golden rules of biblical interpretation is that every verse has a context and must be interpreted in the light of that context. Failure to observe this rudimentary principle has led to some terrible confusions and errors. And another golden rule is this: Scripture is always itself the best interpreter of Scripture. Both rules apply here.

The context, we have already seen, is Christ and the elect in glory. The interpreting Scripture to bear in mind to help us is the great truth of Ephesians 1:4, that the ultimate goal of election is holiness. 'For he chose us in him [that is, God chose us in Christ] before the creation of the world to be holy and blameless in his sight.' So, you see, it is the final result of the cleansing and sanctifying work of the Holy Spirit upon the elect – the final goal and outcome of the whole glorious work of salvation – that explains the language here in verses 4–5. To borrow William Cowper's phrase, we are looking at all the ransomed church of God, saved to sin no more!

Four features of the redeemed are brought out: they did not defile themselves with women, but rather kept themselves pure; they follow the Lamb wherever He goes; they are purchased ones and first-fruit offerings and they are blameless, with no lies or impurities attached to them.

This description should not imply, of course, that all the redeemed ones are men; still less, that they remained celibate all their lives. That is utterly to miss the point. The whole thrust is their complete sanctification – our complete sanctification, something which is never reached in this life, where we are always straining forward, pressing on and in process of being changed into Christ's likeness, but which will be entire and complete in glory.

The reference to sexual purity should be understood in two senses. There is what we might call the literal sense. The Bible cries out for sexual purity. The *root* of the matter is the command: 'Just as he who called you is holy, so be holy in all you do; for it is written, "Be holy, because I am holy"' (1 Peter 1:15–16). The *fruit* of the matter is the uncompromising insistence: 'Flee from sexual immorality . . .

he who sins sexually sins against his own body. Do you not know that your body is a temple of the Holy Spirit, who is in you, whom you have received from God? You are not your own; you were bought at a price. Therefore honour God with your body' (1 Corinthians 6:18–20). We are to offer our bodies 'as living sacrifices, holy and pleasing to God' (Romans 12:1). The *heart* of the matter is the crystal-clear message of 1 Thessalonians 4:7–8: 'For God did not call us to be impure, but to live a holy life. Therefore he who rejects this instruction does not reject man, but God, who gives you his Holy Spirit.' While we are about it, let it be said that Romans 6:11–23 deserves a careful look as well.

This is not some 'take-it or leave-it' extra to the Christian life. It is central. It is crucial. All forms of sexual immorality (adultery, fornication, lustful thoughts or imaginings, mastur-bation, homosexuality, and so on) are forbidden and con-demned by God in His Word. We are to 'live a life worthy of the calling [we] have received' (Ephesians 4:1). 'Do not grieve the Holy Spirit of God, with whom you were sealed for the day of redemption' (Ephesians 4:30).

But there is also what we might call the spiritual sense. That should be understood against the background of Old Testament teaching, where sexual purity often stood for a picture of faithfulness to God, while impurity (adultery) spoke of unfaithfulness. As for the mention of firstfruits in verse 4, Wilson rightly remarks, 'Since the 144,000 are the totality of the redeemed, "firstfruits" cannot here mean that there are more to follow, but carries the more usual sense of an offering to God.'

In summary, then, these first five verses present us with a mouth-watering picture of the redeemed of the Lord. We are to be characterized by nothing less than absolute commit-ment to Christ, wholesale belonging to God and complete truthfulness and purity.

The angels with their messages

We have become used by now to the Revelation's strange pictures, but there are still many more to come before the book is finished. We are now introduced to three angels, each of them having something significant to say.

The first angel (6–7) is seen 'flying in mid-air', and having 'the eternal gospel to proclaim to those who live on the earth'. There is an important tie-up between the end of chapter 14:6 and chapter 7:9: the universality of the elect in terms of the elect gathered from all the earth and the gospel proclaimed to all the earth. That gospel message is summarized in the clarion call to mankind to 'Fear God and give him glory . . . worship him.'

God's judgement hour has come and the right and pre-rogative of judgement is His because He is the Creator of the ends of the earth: He 'made the heavens, the earth, the sea and the springs of water'. He calls His own creation to account. He summons all whom He has made to judgement.

The fact, as we have just noted, that the first angel's message is described as 'the eternal gospel' has caused some to ask just where the gospel message is to be found in it, for these verses look like a wholesale announcement of judgement not tempered in any measure by a declaration of good news. To this we can say two things. First of all we must remember that full-orbed gospel preaching means not only speaking comfortable and encouraging words in setting forth the hope there now is for sinners since Christ died at Calvary. It involves as well the exposing of sin and the warning of judgement for those who reject the message. There is good news and bad news! It was said of John Bradford, a holy servant of Christ who died at the stake at Smithfield in 1555, that in his preaching and evangelistic ministry he spoke 'the thunder of judgement' and 'the music of mercy'.

But notice in the second place that there is no definite article in the original — so the angel proclaims not only 'the eternal gospel', but 'an eternal gospel' or just 'eternal gospel'. In the light of this, the emphasis of the gospel, or good tidings, in the present context is the comfort believers will derive from the knowledge that God is sovereign and supreme, that He is to be feared, glorified and worshipped and that the tide of His judgement is about to rush in. Dr Hoeksema puts it this way: 'This sounds like

gospel in the ears of God's people. Even though it may
seem as if God has relinquished His eternal claim, they may
depend upon it that He shall vindicate it to the end and
that He shall reveal His wrath to the kingdom of Antichrist.'
God's judgements mean His people's deliverance and the
realization of all His promises in which we have rested.

The second angel (8) follows on and pronounces the doom
of Babylon. We shall consider the picture of Babylon in
detail when we come to chapters 17 and 18. Suffice it to
say for now that Babylon in the book of Revelation stands
for the world with all its seductions and charms, the world
reserved for destruction.

What is the message implicit here? Look where the world
is going — and if you belong to the world, look where you
are going with it!

The third angel (9–11) proclaims a similar theme, pro-
nouncing judgement on the worshippers of the beast. The
awful truth is clear. If you choose the world and Satan, you
will perish with the world and Satan. Here and now God's
wrath is mixed with mercy, but the vivid pictures of drinking **'the wine of God's fury'** and being **'tormented with
burning sulphur'** point to the terrible and inescapable reality
of judgement and hell that awaits all 'those who do not
know God and do not obey the gospel of our Lord Jesus'
(2 Thessalonians 1:8).

William Still has some helpful remarks at this point. He
says that 'The eternal fire of God's wrath is described in
extreme physical terms, not merely to shock and horrify,
but also to indicate that the spiritual reality will be far
worse than any earthly fire.' And he adds this necessary
observation: 'The nearer we travel into the heart of the
Eternal, learning that He is "wonderfully kind", the more
we see how justified He is in dealing faithfully with those
who spurn His grace . . . We must begin to think on the
subject from the heavenly standpoint, namely, that the
eternal God in His redemptive work is dealing with fallen
sinners who, apart from grace, are, without exception,
deserving wrath and punishment; else our human sensitivity
to the eternal punishment of the wicked will lead us astray.'

We cannot escape the awful implication of verse 11: hell is as eternal as heaven. And look at the phrase in verse 10, 'in the presence of the holy angels and of the Lamb'. The excruciating agony of the wicked will be increased manifold by their view of the triumph of the Lamb — the One against whom they had made war all their lives.

Before we leave this second scene in the chapter, we have an earnest call (12) and a blessed assurance (13). The call for patient endurance and faithfulness on the part of the saints is reminiscent of chapter 13:10. It is a call which needs to be applied constantly. There is never a day, never a moment, when we do not need to hear it and to heed it. Though remember that, however terrible in this life our sufferings might be, they cannot compare with the very different sufferings of the enemies of God after the judgement. And then come the familiar and precious words of verse 13. What a blessed assurance they impart — the real spiritual blessedness and rest from their labours of those 'who die in the Lord'!

The harvest with its judgements

John began this chapter with 'Then I looked'. And whom did he see? The Lamb, the Lord Jesus Christ, the glorious Victor on behalf of His people, the Lamb who was slain and with His blood purchased men for God, the King of kings and Lord of lords, God's Anointed One, Christ in His fulness of glory and grace.

Now again in verse 14, John says, 'I looked'. And whom did he see this time? Look carefully at the description. Who is it? It is the Lord Jesus Christ again — the same person already described in verse 1, but described now according to different attributes and in a different office: not Saviour but Judge.

This section of the chapter brings us to the end of the world, to the reality of judgement, even though we are still only some two-thirds of the way through the book. Keep in mind once more those principles of progressive parallelism of the visions that we laid down earlier on.

Some commentators have resisted the identification of

the personage of verse 14 with Christ. They urge that it would mean that Christ takes His orders from angels (15), and that His own work is made to appear in the middle of what this angel and that angel were doing. Certainly this is one of the more difficult questions of interpretation in Revelation upon which we must make up our minds, but I shall settle for the traditional identification of chapter 14:14 with Christ. Certainly the picture of 'one "like a son of man"', deriving from Daniel 7:13, is familiarly applied to Christ in the New Testament (and has already been so applied in chapter 1:13), and Jesus often called Himself 'Son of man'. The crown is a mark of the messianic King (look on to 19:12) and the fact that it is golden here reminds us of the sovereign lordship and kingship of Christ.

> The head that once was crowned with thorns
> Is crowned with glory now;
> A royal diadem adorns
> The mighty Victor's brow
> (Thomas Kelly).

And the sharp sickle in His hand is in line with Christ's character as the Judge and Divider of men (cf. Luke 2:34). When John speaks in verse 15 of 'another angel', the contrast is not with the Christ of verse 14, but with the three angels who appeared in verses 6–11.

As this section continues, we see how the earth is reaped and judged. An angel 'came out of the temple' — that is, out of the immediate presence of the holy God. There is a strong feel of Joel 3:13 about the imagery used, as well as Matthew 13:30, 39 in Jesus' parable of the wheat and the weeds. Once again the vividness of the language impresses us: the crushing of the grapes in a winepress being used to describe the judgement of the wicked, and the picture then suddenly changing from what we would have expected (grape juice) to blood in verse 20 — a huge lake of blood spreading out in all directions for some 180 miles, and deep enough for horses to swim in it. We are probably right to think of 'the earth's vine' as symbolizing Christless humanity *en masse*, while 'the clusters of grapes' speak more particularly of individual unbelievers.

Do you remember that desperate question back in chapter 6:17: in the face of God's wrath, 'Who can stand?' Thankfully the answer remains the same while the day of grace continues: those 'who have washed their robes and made them white in the blood of the Lamb' (7:14). All who truly repent of and forsake their sins and call upon the name of the Lord will be saved. But this chapter 14 warns us, and warns us unmistakably, that the judgement of God is on its way. Nothing will hold it up. God has fixed the day. The gospel is not a light-hearted 'take-it or leave-it' offer.

All of which should drive us to searching self-examination, earnest prayer and urgent evangelism.

What will it be for you? A day of triumph or a day of reckoning?

15.
The wrath of God

Please read Revelation 15 and 16

We have arrived at another important sub-division in the book of Revelation. We have already had the opening of the seven seals; then the seventh seal opened up into the blowing of the seven trumpets. Now we come to the pouring out of the seven bowls, described in chapter 15:7 as 'seven golden bowls [A.V., vials] filled with the wrath of God, who lives for ever and ever'. That gives us the clue to the interpretation of chapters 15 and 16. They continue to reveal the judgements of God throughout history, designed to lead men to repentance. But when we get to the seventh bowl (16:17), that's it! 'It is done!' The wrath of God is finished. Judgement has come. The Christless ones (so often warned, so often pricked in their conscience, so often having had the truth of the gospel and the claims of Christ pressed upon them, yet all of this having had no effect), will be plunged finally into the hands of an angry God.

There is a threefold division that we can observe in these chapters: chapter 15 speaks of the reality of God's wrath and the 'context' of God's wrath, while chapter 16 records the pouring out of God's wrath.

1. The reality of God's wrath

God's character, set forth in the Bible, is most wonderfully and exquisitely varied. You have profound summary statements like 'God is love' or 'God is light, and in him there is no darkness at all.' He is 'the eternal God', 'the jealous God', 'the compassionate and gracious God' and 'the God of all

140

comfort'. He is the God who is 'holy, holy, holy'. It is impossible to find one attribute which is the sum of all the others. But there is no doubt as to which aspect of God's character is to the fore in our present section. The answer must be God's wrath. It is mentioned in verses 1 and 7 of chapter 15 and then twice more in chapter 16.

See how chapter 15 opens. John 'saw **in heaven another great and marvellous sign'**. The 'another' is in contrast with the signs he had seen before (cf. 12:1, 3; 13:1, 11; 14:1, 6–11, 14). Once again it is **'great and marvellous'** – awe-inspiring, amazing, wonderful! And what is it? **'Seven angels with the seven last plagues'**, which bring an end to God's wrath. It is complete. It is full.

Then, if we look down to verses 5–8, what else do we find in John's vision? He records that **'In heaven the temple, that is, the tabernacle of the Testimony, was opened.'** This is the only occurrence of this expression, but it would seem likely that the background thought is the Old Testament expression, 'the tent of meeting' (A.V., 'the tabernacle of the congregation') – in other words, a symbol of the very presence of God. Out of the very presence of the holy God – from God Himself – came the seven angels, dazzlingly described in verse 6, and in whose very appearance there is a reflection of God's holiness. They received from the four living creatures (Remember them? Look back to chapter 4) the 'seven golden bowls filled with the wrath of God'. The time has come when the wrath of God is to be poured out upon a sinful, God-hating, Christ-rejecting, rebellious world. What a moment!

Dr Hoeksema has a magnificent paragraph which I must quote here: 'It is one of the most wonderful periods in all the history of the world. It is the eve of the realization of all things, the eve of that moment when God shall appear in all the power of His holiness, when His Word shall appear to be the truth also over the wicked world, when His Name shall appear glorious and victorious over all things. It is the eve of that greatest of all events, for which the hearts of all God's people long and yearn, for which the souls beneath the altar cry day and night without rest. It is the eve of that event when Christ shall appear as the Lamb Who hath been slain, as the victorious King of kings, as the Mighty One

Who has power over all things, as the Anointed One over Zion, His holy place. It is the eve of that event which shall show the futility of all the works of the devil and shall for evermore do away with the kingdom of darkness. It is the most momentous period in the history of the world, the eve of the realization of all God's counsel.'

The whole sense of this is heightened with the language of verse 8. There is no doubting the reality of God's wrath. Romans 1:18 teaches that 'The wrath of God is being revealed from heaven against all the godlessness and wickedness of men who suppress the truth by their wickedness.' This is happening all the time. What this section of the book of Revelation teaches is that 'is being revealed' will one day become 'is finally revealed', 'is revealed once and for all'. In the language of the psalmist, God will have shut up His tender mercies.

Yet there is sometimes confusion over this attribute of God's character. Some people think that to speak of God's wrath at all is to insult God. Some insist that it is to attach to Him an attribute that does not and cannot belong to Him. Some urge that it does not fit in with their idea of God as being nothing but love. So it is worth pausing for a moment at this point to clear up this vital matter.

To speak of God's wrath does not mean that God has passionate and irrational fits of anger and rage, that He loses His temper, flies off the handle or gets beside Himself. That would be to insult Him! What God's wrath does signify is this: because He is holy, He hates all sin and cannot have anything to do with it, and because He hates all sin His anger burns against the sinner. His wrath is His holiness stirred into activity against sin and it leads to His executing a sentence of judgement and punishment upon those who reject the gospel of His grace, focused in the giving of His Son. J. I. Packer rightly affirms that 'Just as God is good to those who trust Him, so He is terrible to those who do not.'[29] And A. W. Pink adds that 'The wrath of God is as much a Divine perfection as is His faithfulness, power or mercy.'[30]

In short, you do not have the God of the Bible if you exclude or refuse to reckon with His wrath!

2. The context of God's wrath

What I mean by this phrase is the 'context' in which the pouring out of God's wrath appears here in Revelation 15 and 16 and, following on from that, the context in which God's wrath in past and contemporary judgements should be seen and the context in which His final Day of Judgement will be seen. For God's wrath does not exist in limbo. It does not just suddenly appear out of the blue. It has a context. As a result, God can never be charged with acting unfairly or with dealing unjustly in any way.

As we look at verses 2—4 of chapter 15, it is a case once more of the sight John saw and the song John heard.

The sight John saw
There are two aspects of it — the sea of glass and the great company of people, both in verse 2.

In the vision of God seated upon His heavenly throne in chapter 4, John observed that 'Before the throne there was what looked like a sea of glass, clear as crystal' (4:6). This time the sea of glass is not 'clear as crystal' but 'mixed with fire'. Glass and fire are a strange combination. I am sure that we are right, with Dr Hendriksen, to see this combination as a symbol of God's transparent righteousness (the sea of glass) revealed in judgements on the wicked (mixed with fire). We shall see that this links in with the song of verse 4.

As for the great company of people who were victorious over the beast, this victorious, praising and God-glorifying gathering is surely not to be restricted to those who have endured the thick of the battle, the most burning heat of the day, in the end times, but rather is descriptive of all the saints of God, all the church of Christ. Which means that in this vision, John saw you and me, dear fellow believer!

The song John heard
Its *accompaniment* was on 'harps given them by God' — another lovely reminder of God's sovereign grace in salvation. They (we) would never be enjoying this victory, would never be singing this song and would never have

remained faithful and persevered to the end, were it not for the free, glorious and continuing grace of God. Even the harps are given by Him!

Its *title* is 'the song of Moses the servant of God and the song of the Lamb'. This is not to be taken as implying two songs (one of Moses and the other a different one of the Lamb), but one song — another firm reminder of the unity of the Testaments, the oneness of God's people in every age and the fact that the Lord Jesus Christ is for all, over all and in all. A prayerful meditation upon Ephesians 2:11–22 and Galatians 3:26–29 may be profitable here. All God's victories are the victories of the same Redeemer and for the same church, so it is fitting that the whole body of the redeemed should sing the same song together.

And its *words* are very reminiscent of the wonderful occasion in Exodus 15 when, after God's mighty deliverance of His people through the Red Sea and His destruction of their enemies in that same sea, Moses and the Israelites sang a song of praise to the Lord. Four strands can be seen quite clearly in the song — four great and glorious themes are struck:

1. Great and marvellous are God's deeds.
2. Just and true are God's ways.
3. Fearful and glorious is God's name.
4. Holy and righteous are God's acts.

You and I are still in this world. There are many things we do not understand, many things that perplex us, many things that we can so easily misinterpret or fail to interpret at all. This is so at every level — internationally, nationally, in church life, in family life and personally. Yet even now by faith we can sing the song of Moses and the Lamb because of the fundamental and abiding truth of those four themes that we have just identified. They are always true!

We need a larger perspective on history than we can obtain merely by viewing our own limited life-span. We need a larger perspective on God's ways and purposes than only what we see Him doing in our own day, our own cities or our own church. The truths of this song show us where we must stand right now; they give us the true context in which to understand God, and not least His wrath and judgements. Even now, then, we may hear and sing this great song of the redeemed, even now as we walk by faith and not by sight. And all the time we can be looking forward to that glorious day when, delivered from sin and oppression, delivered from the enemy who is always on our tail, and set free in heaven truly to glorify the God of our salvation, we shall be able to sing this song together as we have never sung it before!

> Awake, and sing the song
> Of Moses and the Lamb;
> Wake every heart and every tongue,
> To praise the Saviour's name
> > (William Hammond).

3. The pouring out of God's wrath

Whereas chapter 15 sets the scene, chapter 16 provides the action. The seven bowls of wrath are now actually poured out, but notice from verse 1 that even though the angels had already received the bowls, the pouring itself had to wait for the explicit command of God.

The seven bowls divide quite naturally into 'four plus three'. The first four all relate to different spheres of nature:

First bowl – on the land (2).

Second bowl – on the sea (3).

Third bowl – on the rivers and springs of water (4–7).

Fourth bowl – on the sun (8–9).

The latter three all relate to vital and cataclysmic matters at the very end of the last days:

Fifth bowl – the attack upon Satan's throne (10–11).

Sixth bowl – the battle of Armageddon (12–16).

Seventh bowl – the final judgement, with the total destruction of the enemy's empire of evil (17–21).

Let us look at each of the bowls in turn.

The first bowl is poured out upon the land and results in 'ugly and painful sores' breaking out. These plagues generally remind us at various points of the plagues God sent upon Egypt during the days of Israel's captivity recorded in

Exodus (as did the early trumpet blasts of chapter 8). The land (and the other parts of the natural world mentioned in the following verses) is to be taken literally and not spiritualized. The picture is of the whole earth being diseased — its soil, its crops, its mineral resources, and so on — all those things upon which people depend for their very existence. It is a picture of a world of universal misery; the sores cover all manner of diseases, which in any given instance may be for one person a warning (that they might have space to repent) and for another person the thing which carries them away. The specific statement that the sores **'broke out on the people who had the mark of the beast and worshipped his image'** reminds us that although God's judgements necessarily involve His people, they are not judgements upon His people. All our judgement has already been borne in our place by the Lord Jesus Christ.

The second bowl is poured out upon the sea, which is turned into blood. It becomes foul, offensive and poisonous. Everything to do with the sea (another great source of man's livelihood) comes to a final standstill. Included here are not only the maritime disasters and ocean dangers already pictured with the trumpets, but the death of all sea life and the end of all commerce and trade.

You can already see more of the practical outworking of the ground-rule principle of progressive parallelism. When the seals were opened, one-fourth of things was affected. When the trumpets were blown, one-third became the symbolic figure, as we remarked at the time. There was an increase! But now that the bowls are being poured out, there is no mention of any mathematical fraction. The whole of everything is affected, for God's wrath is complete.

So while, as with the seals and the trumpets, the bowls are in measure applicable throughout history, yet in their fullest and their universal character they still belong to the future, to the end time itself.

The third bowl is poured out upon the rivers and springs of water, which also turn to blood. Here are the inland waterways, the water systems and water supplies, the reservoirs — again, all so vital for the maintenance of life. All the comforts and necessities of life are being taken away — gradually, bit by bit, and then finally. Life will become increasingly unbearable, until finally 'that's it'.

It is instructive to observe a couple of tie-ups: verse 5 with chapter 15:3—4, and verse 7 with chapter 6:9—10. The justice of God in punishing those who will not repent and the righteousness of God in all His judgements are again to the fore. Never can a word be said, a charge levelled, or a finger pointed against Him. Those who have rejected the gospel will receive (it has to be said) precisely what they deserve.

The fourth bowl is poured out upon the sun, that great light-giver and heavenly luminary, now turned into service for the wrath of God. What a terrible picture of people being scorched by its heat! We are aware, even now, of the potentially fatal effects of sunstroke and the scorching of drought-stricken lands — so how much more terrible will it be at the end time for those who will not repent! Yet what cause have we to praise God, if we are Christians, for the comforting truth of chapter 7:16 in the light of all this!

It goes without saying, of course, that we must proceed cautiously in our interpreting of verses such as these, in respect of the fact that we do not know exactly how God will bring these matters to pass. We must not pry too deeply — sufficient for us that He has told us that He will do them. Oh, that any even reading this book who still need to repent from their sins and turn to Christ would do so, while the door of grace remains open and the day of salvation is still here!

As to the remaining bowls, each of them sketches in themes which continue and are amplified in chapters 17—20 of Revelation, so we do not need to say everything that can be said right now.

The fifth bowl pictures God's wrath being poured out upon **'the throne of the beast'**. The beast must be the character mentioned at the beginning of chapter 13 — the picture there was of evil government and the regimes of Antichrist.

The final overthrow of this whole system is now recorded. To be sure, there are many such falls in history (whether, for example, ancient Pharaoh from the Exodus days, the death of Herod in Acts 12:21—23, or the fall of men like Hitler and Mao Tse Tung), but at the end time the whole business, the whole system, the whole edifice of worldly government in rebellion against God will collapse and be destroyed (remember 11:15!). To this end, notice the plunging into darkness imagery, the agonies, the cursing and the blaspheming — and, still, the refusal to repent.

The sixth bowl pictures the battle of Armageddon, described again in the second part of chapter 19. A word on Armageddon itself. The word actually means 'mountain of Megiddo', and there is a clear Old Testament allusion behind it. Do you recall Deborah and Barak in Judges 4—5? It was on the battlefield of Megiddo that they enjoyed a great victory over the Canaanites, who, under their King Jabin and his General Sisera, had been opposing the Israelites vigorously. What this Armageddon of the book of Revelation symbolizes is God's final mighty clash with all evil governments and powers, with all the forces that are hostile to Him, His Christ and His people.

The dragon, the beast and the false prophet make a re-appearance from chapters 12—13, and Dr Hendriksen remarks helpfully that 'When the world, under the leadership of Satan, anti-Christian government and anti-Christian religion is gathered against the church for the final battle, and the need is greatest; when God's children, opposed on every side, cry for help; then suddenly, dramatically, Christ will appear to deliver His people. The final tribulation and the appearance of Christ on the clouds of glory to deliver His people, that is Armageddon.'

It is important to grasp that. The further details of the vision (the drying up of the Euphrates River, the gathering of the kings from the East, and the three evil spirits looking like frogs) merely add to the total picture of the increasing wickedness of the world, the loathsome and repulsive character of the devil's ideas and plans and the increasing marshalling of all the forces of evil (physical and spiritual) against the Lord Jesus Christ.

But Christ is coming, verse 15 assures us, and our business is to be ready and awake, clothed in Christ's justifying and sanctifying righteousness, which alone can protect us on that day or any other day.

The seventh bowl pictures the final judgement itself. We have virtually been there before in the visions of the book, and while this is the fullest description so far, the final account is still reserved for chapter 20. Notice that the bowl is poured out 'into the air' — what a potent symbol to declare that everything will perish! The very atmosphere itself will be filled with the wrath of God, and the cry will be heard: 'It is done!'

Have we not heard that cry before? A different Greek word is used in John 19:30 from the word used here in verse 17, but we cannot miss the parallel. In the instance in John's Gospel, the Lord Jesus Christ was announcing the triumphant conclusion of His work for our salvation. Nothing more remains to be done. The Lord Jesus Christ has done all, accomplished all, performed all for us! We are complete in Him! And on the last day, God's wrath in judgement will also be complete. The seven golden bowls will be emptied completely, the wrath of God will be fully declared and will have taken its course. Nothing will be held back. This does not, however, detract one jot from the eternity of God's wrath in hell; in that terrible respect, God's wrath is infinite and never comes to an end.

And so there follows an alarming picture of the catastrophe of that day (18–21), involving collapsing cities, fleeing islands, disappearing mountains and even one-hundred-pound weight hailstones. But still no repentance.

A trio of applications

Before we leave these two chapters, it is worth gathering up three practical applications.
1. There is no help, no comfort and no ground of confidence or security to be found anywhere in all creation. The whole earth will be filled with the wrath of God. Men will be left with nowhere at all to run and hide.

2. There is a repeated emphasis upon the hardening of the hearts of individual sinners as a result of these plagues. What a reminder that only the free and sovereign grace of God can break a sinner and change him! If that glorious grace of God does not enter our hearts and if the glorious Word of God does not call us to Him, then . . . Here is a call to prayer and a call to evangelism, for the glory of God.

3. Yet there is massive comfort for the saints as well in these hair-raising chapters. We have had several times previously in the book a call to patience and endurance. God is on the throne. He has full control. Vengeance belongs to Him alone. And this means (if I may put it like this) that we never need to fear for God. He will glorify Himself! Both in the destruction of the wicked and in the salvation of His people He will glorify Himself. Be sure and be thankful that you belong to His people! For between us sinners and the thunderclouds of God's wrath there stands the cross of the Lord Jesus Christ, 'Jesus, who rescues us from the coming wrath' (1 Thessalonians 1:10). This is the meaning behind that grand word 'propitiation'. Christ is our wrath-bearer. There is hope for the hopeless, shelter from the storm, refuge for the terrified and life for the condemned to be found in Him — but only in Him! If we belong to Christ, the wrath of God will never touch us, for He has faced it and had it poured out upon Him at Calvary. Well did Toplady pen these matchless lines:

> If Thou hast my discharge procured,
> And freely in my room endured
>   The whole of wrath divine;
> Payment God cannot twice demand,
> First at my bleeding Surety's hand,
>   And then again at mine.

16.
Babylon

Please read Revelation 17 and 18

Does it not thrill you when you continue to discover how one portion of Scripture is a commentary upon another? Do you know what were A. W. Pink's last words as he lay in his bed in his house in Stornoway dying? 'The Scriptures explain themselves.'[31] Yes, they do! And the two chapters now before us yield a choice example of this. The subject of chapters 17 and 18, which belong very intimately together, is Babylon. You can divide the material up quite clearly in the following way:

1. The character of Babylon (17:1–6).
2. The history of Babylon (17:7–18).
3. The fall of Babylon (18).

This is not the first time in the book of Revelation that we have met Babylon, nor the first time that its fall has been announced. That provides us with yet another caution against any strictly chronological interpretation of these visions. Back in chapter 14:8 we read the words of one of the high-flying angels: 'Fallen! Fallen is Babylon the Great, which made all the nations drink the maddening wine of her adulteries.' That was followed up in chapter 16:19 with the statement: 'God remembered Babylon the Great and gave her the cup filled with the wine of the fury of his wrath.' And now two whole chapters are devoted to Babylon. And all this material is really a commentary upon, or an exposition of, 1 John 2:15–17. Hence the remarks above about one Scripture being a commentary upon another, and so the Scriptures being self-explanatory. Once we grasp that here, this section becomes far plainer to understand.

Here are the apostle John's words from his first letter: 'Do not love the world or anything in the world. If anyone loves the world, the love of the Father is not in him. For everything in the world — the cravings of sinful man, the lust of his eyes and the boasting of what he has and does — comes not from the Father but from the world. The world and its desires pass away, but the man who does the will of God lives for ever.'

1. The character of Babylon

See what happened. One of the seven angels who had been pouring out the bowls of wrath came to John with a message. The angel desired to show John '**the punishment of the great prostitute, who sits on many waters**', the one with whom '**the kings of the earth committed adultery and the inhabitants of the earth were intoxicated with the wine of her adulteries**' (1—2).

So off John went at the angel's invitation, '**in the Spirit into a desert**'. And what a ghastly sight was waiting for him when he got there! He saw a woman — but what a woman! She is very gaudily described in verses 3—4: '**sitting on a scarlet beast that was covered with blasphemous names and had seven heads and ten horns**'. Her clothes were '**purple and scarlet**', she was '**glittering with gold, precious stones and pearls**', and '**she held a golden cup in her hand, filled with abominable things and the filth of her adulteries**'. How absolutely foul! But that is not all. There was a title written upon her forehead (5):

Mystery
Babylon the Great
The Mother of Prostitutes
and of the Abominations of the Earth

But that is still not all! She was drunk — but see what with: '**Drunk with the blood of the saints, the blood of those who bore testimony to Jesus**' (6). We are hardly surprised to read John's remark: '**When I saw her, I was greatly astonished.**' Which of us would not have been?

Indeed, it was surely enough to have made him ill, let alone astonished!

Now, what is the meaning of this symbol? The character of Babylon is set forth here in full colour, but what does it all add up to? Many answers have been given! Some believe the reference is to the literal city of Babylon; others favour the unfaithful or apostate church in general, or the Roman Catholic Church in particular. But those interpretations narrow the symbol down too restrictively. Some of these elements may be part of the picture (the apostate church and the whole edifice of Romanism are certainly in there somewhere), but the picture itself is far bigger than any or all of them.

I stand by the earlier interpretation given when remarking upon chapter 14:8. Babylon in the book of Revelation stands for the world with all its seductions and charms, the world reserved for destruction. Note these quotations from Hendriksen. Babylon stands for 'that which allures, tempts, seduces and draws people away from God', and as such, 'it reminds us of pleasure-mad, arrogant, presumptuous Babylon of old'. Just think back to Nimrod's kingdom (Genesis 10:10) and the desire behind Babel that he built: 'Come, let us build ourselves a city, with a tower that reaches to the heavens, so that we may make a name for ourselves' (Genesis 11:4).

That is why I urged at the beginning that the whole picture of Babylon here is a commentary upon those verses from 1 John. Think particularly of 1 John 2:16, with its mention of vital characteristics of worldliness: 'the cravings of sinful man, the lust of his eyes and the boasting of what he has and does'. This symbol of the prostitute Babylon is the very embodiment of all that. To turn to Dr Hendriksen again, Babylon is 'the concentration of the luxury, vice and glamour of the world'. A painted lady!

2. The history of Babylon

What the rest of chapter 17 gives us is a brief review (or overview) of Babylon's history — a reminder of some of its typical manifestations in history. First of all, read the verses

through again, then come back to verse 7 and follow through
the angel's explanation to John of 'the mystery of the
woman and of the beast she rides'. What are the chief details?

v. 8. The beast 'once was, now is not, and will come up
out of the Abyss and go to his destruction'.

vv. 9—11. The beast's seven heads are seven hills and also
seven kings. Of those seven kings, 'five have fallen, one is,
the other has not yet come'. The beast itself is an eighth
king who 'belongs to the seven and is going to his
destruction'.

vv. 12—18. The beast's ten horns are also ten kings —
kings who 'have not yet received a kingdom', but will receive
authority along with the beast for one hour, kings whose
express purpose it is to 'make war against the Lamb', but
kings who will be overcome by the Lamb and His followers.
Then in the last part of this paragraph, a sort of 'self-
destruction' seems to be described as Babylon apparently
turns in upon itself.

Now what should we make of all this? Before we begin,
just stop and remember again one of the principles of interpretation which we have sought to follow all along: don't
miss the wood for the trees. Some symbols require interpretation, while others do not need to be dealt with in
such a specific or individual manner, but are there, if you
like, for the total effect. Here we go!

The woman was on the scarlet beast. It 'once was'. Tie
that up with the five kings already fallen, and you have a
typical manifestation of the 'world' in the kingdoms of
Old Babylonia, Assyria, New Babylonia, Medo-Persia and
Greco-Macedonia: kingdoms of the ancient world that have
been and gone.

The beast 'now is not'. Tie that up with the king who is —
in other words, though plenty of manifestations of Babylon
have already disappeared without trace ('the beast now is
not') yet Babylon is still alive and well and to be seen in
John's present day ('one is'). That is an allusion to the
empire of Rome which was spawning out in every direction
in the hard days of persecution through which John himself
was living.

And the beast 'yet will come'. And see from where: 'out
of the Abyss and go to his destruction'. Babylon has this

habit of bouncing back throughout history. Inspired from the very pit of hell, back she comes again and again with her same old make-up, same old seductions and same old beckonings to keep people in slavery to sin. Tie that up with the king who is yet to come and will remain for a little while, which is best understood as a collective reference to the whole host of worldly, Babylonish, anti-Christian governments and regimes which will appear on the scene of world history between the fall of Rome and the final onslaughting empire of Antichrist which will oppose the church just prior to Christ's return in glory at the end of the age.

But the beast will be destroyed! Babylon will fall! And that defeat will be at the hands of the only One to whom the titles 'Lord of lords and King of kings' belong — the Lord Jesus Christ!

And, as chapter 17 closes, we are reminded of how the world increasingly will turn in on and against itself. As the end time approaches and as the deluded and imprisoned inhabitants of the world find all their dreams of the world delivering all the promised goods fail, their hearts become more and more hardened against God and it is too late to repent. Leon Morris captures the very sense of it when he writes, 'Wicked men are not just one happy band of brothers. Being wicked, they give way to jealousy and hatred. At the climax their mutual hatreds will result in mutual destruction.' Even in the space of our own lifetime we can see abundant evidence of this principle of the world versus the world, Babylon versus Babylon. What is in one moment is out the next — styles of fashion, music and architecture come and go; heroes of politics, trade unions, sport and show business rise and fall; *coup* follows *coup*, and so on. It is, quite literally, the way of the world.

3. The fall of Babylon

How utterly hollow and miserable the idea that 'This world is everything there is,' will prove to be! People are finding that out all the time. There are disappointed, disillusioned, broken and hopeless people around us on every side. They

have been taken in by the beast and seduced by the prostitute. They have gone after those things which they can
taste, see and measure right now and remain ignorant of
Christ and spiritual blessings. And what do they have?
What will they have? What will they be left with? Nothing.

> I tried the broken cisterns, Lord,
> But ah! The waters failed!
> Even as I stopped to drink they fled
> And mocked me as I wailed.

Chapter 18 divides into two parts: Babylon's obituary
(1—8) and Babylon's lament (9—24).

Babylon's obituary

John saw yet 'another angel coming down from heaven',
an angel with authority and splendour. And with a mighty
voice this angel uttered again the cry already heard some
chapters previously: 'Fallen! Fallen is Babylon the Great!'
The world that thought it was at such a great height has
fallen to such a great depth. The world that claimed to
have everything on offer is left empty and dry. The
description in verses 2—3 says it all.

Then notice verses 5—7. Babylon's sins are 'piled up to
heaven'. That is a statement which admits a great fulness of
interpretation. Clearly the actual scope and quantity of the
world's sin is spoken of here — it reaches to heaven itself,
as it were. And because sin's primary description is anti-
God, disobedience to God, the casting off and rejection
of God, even to the point of seeking to prove that God
does not even exist, then the sense of 'against heaven' is
also included.

But all that sin will be punished, and punished 'double'
(6). That 'double' means not so much the sense of twice
as much punishment as there had been sin (a 'double dose'
of punishment), but rather (7) the exact counterpart in
punishment of all that Babylon's sin has earned her. And
all this mighty and terrible judgement will come upon her
suddenly. 'Therefore in one day her plagues will overtake
her' (8). One day sitting boastfully as a queen, the next
day down in the dirt, fallen, ruined, never to rise again.

Babylon's lament

There is a most pathetic tone to this lament and it has a double edge to it. For a start, all those who belonged to Babylon, all those who put all their eggs in Babylon's basket, all those who gained the whole world, but in the process lost their souls, are in agony and grief at Babylon's fall. Their best friend has gone. Their (as they thought) great hope and guaranteed satisfaction is ruined. Their life-support machine has been switched off. There is nothing left of all that they were counting upon. And that in itself is a bitter enough blow for them.

But there is this double edge. For Scripture teaches so plainly that while Babylon will one day fall ('The world and its desires pass away', 1 John 2:17) yet people live on, and those who do not spend eternity with Christ among all the myriad delights of glory must spend eternity separated from Christ in all the agonies of hell, having lost (this is the particular point in the present context) everything which in life they thought was worth having. Babylon has abandoned them once and for all, but the wrath of God abides upon them for ever. Oh, solemn thought! So these two things go together: the fall of Babylon the Great, and the punishment, destruction, bitterness, hopelessness, collapse and ruin of all those who looked to Babylon.

The *kings of the earth* lament (9—10). All the kings, princes, rulers, governments, statesmen and politicians who, having received power and responsibility from God, have abused it, have not acknowledged God, have used it for their own ends and to exalt themselves — all those who for the price of 'votes' have abandoned or relaxed various laws or moral standards and allowed an ever-increasing range of vile and permissive practices — will mourn and lament. Included here is the whole miserable business of the 'state church' and the Roman Catholic/Vatican State tie-up.

The *merchants* lament (11—17). All that delighted them is suddenly destroyed. All the business and the cargoes for which they lived and upon which they set their hearts have failed them. Well did the Lord Jesus Christ exhort us, 'Do not store up for yourselves treasures on earth . . . But store up for yourselves treasures in heaven . . . For where your treasure is, there your heart will be also' (Matthew 6:19—21).

The *sea-going men* lament (17—20), for they are ruined too. These are taken by some to stand for the sightseers who never actually had a home in Babylon, but visited from time to time to experiment, taste and enjoy what Babylon had to offer. In other words, those who, let us say, esteemed the Christian moral code, reckoned to lead the right sort of life, 'believed in God', but were still at the end of the day separate from Christ and firmly attached to the world.

And finally, *all who had anything to do with Babylon* lament (21—24). Look what John saw this time: 'A mighty angel picked up a boulder the size of a large millstone and threw it into the sea.' There follows, quite frankly, a terrible picture of what life will be like in hell, the eternal Babylon. Everything will be stripped away. Nothing will remain to give the least shred of enjoyment or satisfaction. Follow the verses through.

There will be no music or entertainment in hell (22). What price now the star billings, the neon lights, the hysterical adulation of the fans? There will be no beautiful melodies in hell, no lush orchestrations, no fine choirs, no musical instruments to delight ear and heart or to soothe the troubled spirit.

The world's skills will have departed as well (22). No arts and crafts, no lovely creations, no exquisite paintings, no beauty or colour.

There will be no light in hell (23). That probably includes two things: no light of wisdom and knowledge, no intellectual debate, no sharpening of minds; and nothing of what the apostle Paul speaks of in Philippians 4:8, nothing noble, right or pure, nothing lovely or admirable, nothing excellent or praiseworthy. How often light in Scripture represents holiness and purity! So 'God is light'. But everything to do with light will have been removed.

And every single token of worldly joy will be absent in hell (23), represented here under the symbol of the bridegroom and the bride — no love, no affection, no delight, no glory, no precious human relationships. Nothing. Look back to that awful statement in verse 21: 'never to be found again'.

How should we leave a passage such as this?

Firstly, with the importance of the call of chapter 18:4 engraved upon our beings. 'Come out of her, my people, so that you will not share in her sins, so that you will not receive any of her plagues.' Never forget that 'This world in its present form is passing away' (1 Corinthians 7:31). Do not be taken in by worldliness. Remember James 4:4: 'You adulterous people, don't you know that friendship with the world is hatred towards God? Anyone who chooses to be a friend of the world becomes an enemy of God.' Do not let the devil's beckonings and Babylon's supposed pleasures ensnare you! John Newton reminds us that:

> Fading is the worldling's pleasure,
> All his boasted pomp and show!
> Solid joys and lasting treasure
> None but Zion's children know.

Secondly, bless God that you are one of Zion's children! See what He has saved you from — all the things of death, destruction and despair, and He has given you instead:

> Pardon for sin, and a peace that endureth,
> Thy own dear presence to cheer and to guide;
> Strength for today and bright hope for tomorrow,
> Blessings all mine, with ten thousand beside!
>
> (T. O. Chisholm).

And all exclusively because of His grace towards you in the Lord Jesus Christ!

And finally, the question is pressed upon us yet again by the book of Revelation: how much do we really care for the lost? How much does it trouble us whether our families and friends are saved or not? We need to speak humbly and earnestly to people about the false and deceitful claims of Babylon and, in contrast, all the glories that are found in the Lord Jesus Christ.

17.
Jesus, Lamb and King

Please read Revelation 19

After chapters 15—18, it is with no small measure of relief and delight that we come to the beginning of chapter 19. The sun seems to be shining brightly again! Two mighty events are now brought before us: the wedding of the Lamb (1—10) and the battle of Armageddon (11—21), and the great thrust of each of them is the glory, majesty and power of the Lord Jesus Christ, triumphant with His people and victorious over all His enemies.

Yet the teaching of the immediately preceding chapters is not suddenly forgotten, for as chapter 19 opens, and as a prelude to, and context for, what it reveals, we have two things. In verses 1—3 John 'heard what sounded like the roar of a great multitude in heaven shouting'. Their shouts of praise were songs of glory to God over the destruction of Babylon. Glorious hallelujahs were called forth quite spontaneously from heaven, and so shall it be! Nothing should delight the servants of God more than God getting glory to Himself! Well do we sing, 'To God be the glory! Great things He hath done!' Then in verses 4—6 the worshipping and singing continue. All the hallelujahs of heaven seem to be let loose. Imagine all the oceans and mighty waterfalls, all the choirs and all the thunders of the world, going strong at the same time, and even then you are only just beginning to imagine a fraction of what those paeans of worship and praise to God will sound like at the Last Day!

Just by the way, we can pick up here a helpful hint on what still remains a problem sometimes for Christians, however earnest or mature. The problem can be stated like

this: 'How shall I really be able to enjoy heaven if some
of my loved ones and friends are not there, but have gone
to hell? Surely it will be impossible.' Obviously the matter
is a delicate and sensitive one. But here in chapter 19 we see
clearly an unreserved glorying in God and an unreserved
happiness in Him right on the very occasion of the fall of
Babylon and God's judgement upon the world. So the clue
we would draw to help us is this. We shall be so absolutely
overjoyed at the full and firm declaration of the sovereign
glory and justice and rule of God (**'Hallelujah! For our
Lord God Almighty reigns'**) and so thoroughly taken up
with the view of Christ and the prospect of hitherto unknown depths of intimacy and fellowship with Him (**'Let
us rejoice and be glad and give him glory! For the wedding
of the Lamb has come'**) that all else will, quite literally, be
blotted out.

And so we come to the first of these two great events
that are presented symbolically in this chapter.

1. The wedding of the Lamb

Let us focus in turn upon the Bridegroom, the bride and
the wedding day itself.

The Bridegroom
It is essential to a wedding day to have a bridegroom and
although the actual word does not appear here it is quite
clear that there is a bridegroom and that that Bridegroom
is the Lamb! He is mentioned in verses 7 and 9. We know
that there are many names given in Scripture to the Lord
Jesus Christ — indeed 'Bridegroom' is one of them (John
3:27—30) — but perhaps this name, 'the Lamb', takes us
closer and deeper into the heart of the person and work of
Christ than any other name. It points to His saving work —
'the Lamb of God who takes away the sin of the world', to
use John the Baptist's phrase. And it is a familiar title in
the book of Revelation (look again at 5:6—8, 12; 7:9, 10,
14, 17; 14:1, along with references to 'the Lamb's book
of life' and 'the book of life belonging to the Lamb that
was slain from the creation of the world'). And now we come

to this great, glorious, climactic moment: the wedding, the marriage supper, of the Lamb.

And the reason why the Bridegroom is designated as the Lamb on His wedding day is this: under this name, supremely, is set forth His uniqueness and glory and the character in which He has revealed Himself to us, demonstrated His love for us and called forth from our hearts and lives a returning and responsive love.

Whenever we read of the Lord Jesus Christ as the Lamb we are reminded again that He is our Substitute, who died for our sins, in our place, upon Calvary's cross. Under that character we first looked to Him and were saved. Is that not true? Which of us loved Him until we saw His wounds and His blood? And that is the character He wears still, with 'those wounds yet visible above, in beauty glorified'. And when we come to enter heaven and live there, we shall still view Him in that central character — the one everlasting sacrifice for sin, the best beloved of our souls. Anne Ross Cousin has it exactly right once more:

> The bride eyes not her garment
> But her dear bridegroom's face;
> I will not gaze at glory,
> But on my King of grace;
> Not at the crown He giveth,
> But on His pierced hand:
> The Lamb is all the glory
> Of Immanuel's land.

The bride

It is just as essential to a wedding to have a bride! The bride is referred to here in verses 7 and 8, as well as by implication in the phrase in verse 9: **'those who are invited'**. Who is the bride? Quite certainly, from what we know of the consistency of Scripture upon this subject, she is the church (the true church) of Christ, the whole company of believers, the complete and gathered in elect people of God. And mark this! That includes you and me if we belong to the Saviour, however much we may sometimes be wrestling with all our sins and doubts and fears! Remember those lines:

> The church's one foundation
> Is Jesus Christ, her Lord;
> She is His new creation
> By water and the word;
> From heaven He came and sought her
> To be His holy bride,
> With His own blood He bought her,
> And for her life He died
>   (Samuel J. Stone).

So the bride at the wedding of the Lamb is His church. And here the emphasis falls upon the readiness, the preparedness, of the bride. Any bride desires to make herself ready for her 'big day'; she does not just turn up in any old condition, not having bothered! She wants to look her best. So here, then, is this emphasis upon the readiness and preparedness of the bride, which straight away recalls to our minds that wonderful passage, Ephesians 5:25—27. It is the preparedness of sanctification, that great work which does not have its completion in us, either individually or collectively, until glory, but will then be complete indeed. It is the eradication of all our sin, the work that the Lord Jesus Christ will have done for us, to us and in us by His Holy Spirit, whom John Owen called 'the great Beautifier of souls'.

It is the complete forming of Christ in us. Do you remember how Paul agonized for that in the lives of the Galatians? (Galatians 4:19.) In this respect, notice the statement in verse 8 about that 'fine linen, bright and clean . . . given her to wear' — the gift of sovereign grace! That 'fine linen stands for the righteous acts [literally, righteousnesses] of the saints'. The meaning is that we shall be arrayed completely, head to foot, in Christ's righteousness, covered through and through with the beauty of holiness. The practical evidence of this is the righteous acts of the saints — our actual deeds as, having been saved by God's grace alone through faith in Christ, we do those 'good works, which God prepared in advance for us to do' (Ephesians 2:10). So our fundamental righteousness in Christ and the confirming proof of it in our righteous acts are, very appropriately, gathered together here. But remember that Christ Himself (1 Corinthians 1:30), not our righteous acts following upon our conversion, constitutes the sole grounds of our confidence before God. What a gorgeous bridal gown we shall wear! The Lord Jesus Christ will see in us, at last, the fruit of all the travail of His soul and be perfectly satisfied.

And there is one more emphasis as well: the complete unity of the church. Because not until the people of God are one as the Father and the Son are one (John 17:11) shall the bride be ready. Here is true evangelical unity, not that so-called unity of the ecumenical movement and so on, but the true, genuine unity in the Lord Jesus Christ of all those 'born of His Spirit, washed in His blood'. Christ will make His people one — and how wonderful that will be!

The wedding day

'Blessed are those who are invited to the wedding supper of the Lamb!' Free grace again! What a day to look forward to — we shall never have been to a wedding like this before! *It will be a day of the glorious fulfilment of all God's purposes for His church and His own glory.* The betrothal of Christ and His church took place not in time but in eternity, when the Father gave us to the Son in the covenant of grace. He will not have lost a single one of us!

It will be a day of home-coming. You know how it is when you have been away from home and loved ones — how good it is to get home! How much better it will be to arrive safely in heaven! This world is not our home. We are citizens of heaven even now, but, oh, what will it be to be there?

It will be a day of mutually intimate communion. How delightful it will be for the Bridegroom and the bride to be united on that day! He will be welcoming us, singing love songs over us, showing us the endless delights He has been preparing for us and we shall gladly follow Him wherever He goes, keeping our gaze fixed upon Him. We shall be made like Him and we shall see Him as He is. Faith will have vanished into sight. Samuel Rutherford once described himself as 'hungry in waiting for the marriage supper of the Lamb'. And that lovely martyr mentioned earlier in the book, John Bradford, turned his head to the young believer, John Leaf, who was tied with him to the stake at Smithfield, ready to be burned, and uttered those matchless words: 'Be of good comfort, brother; for we shall have a merry supper with the Lord this night.'

And so it really goes without saying that *it will be a day of immense joy and living 'happily ever after'*. Unlike fairy stories, this will be real — the day for which the Bridegroom has been waiting; the day for which the people of Christ have been longing; the day even for which the whole of creation has been groaning and travailing. All this is well pictured in the supper feast.

In Jewish wedding ceremonies[32] the marriage feast follows a lengthy period of betrothal, during which the groom and bride have lived separately from one another, and can then go on for quite a time. For the true church of Christ, the joy will last for ever.

The apostle John was so overwhelmed with all this that he fell at the feet of the angel who had been speaking to him and made the mistake of worshipping him. But, quite rightly, the angel would not have it. God alone is to be worshipped. The angel has come not on his own account or to get glory for himself. Rather his concern is to speak of and set forth Christ — his is the **'testimony of Jesus'** and that testimony is **'the spirit of prophecy'**. In other words, Christ is Himself the sum and substance of all prophecy, the focus and centre of all Scripture. He is the Revealer and the Revealed!

Let us leave this section with a most helpful quotation which Spurgeon employs in his sermon notes on chapter 19:9: 'We dare not say that our Lord will love us more than He loves us now, but He will indulge His love for us more; He will manifest it more, we shall see more of it, we shall understand it better; it will appear to us as though He loves us more. He will lay open His whole heart and soul to us, with all its feelings, and secrets, and purposes, and allow us to know them, as far at least as we can understand them, and it will conduce to our happiness to know them. The love of this hour will be the perfection of love. This marriage feast will be the feast, the triumph of love — the exalted Saviour showing to the whole universe that He loves us to the utmost bound love can go, and we loving Him with a fervour, a gratitude, an adoration, a delight,

that are new even in heaven. The provisions made by Him
for our enjoyment will astonish us. Conceive of a beggar
taken for the first time to a splendid monarch's table, and
this at a season of unusual splendour and rejoicing. How
would he wonder at the magnificence he would see around
him, and the profusion of things prepared for his grati-
fication; some altogether new to him, and others in an
abundance and an excellence he had never thought of! So
will it be with us in heaven. We shall find it a feast and a
monarch's feast. It will have delights for us, of which we
have no conception; and the pleasures we anticipate in it
will be far higher and more abundant than our highest
expectations have ever gone. We shall have a provision
made for us, which will befit, not our rank and condition,
but the rank and condition, the greatness, the magnificence,
of a glorious God.'[33]

2. The battle of Armageddon

Chapter 19 is certainly a chapter of contrasts! Our attention
is turned now from the wedding celebrations aspect of
the glory and victory of Christ to a very different aspect
of that glory and victory. Here we are at the battle of
Armageddon. We have already come across this battle in
chapter 16:12—16 under the symbol of the pouring out of
the sixth bowl. We described it then as the final tribulation
and the appearance of Christ on clouds of glory to deliver
His people. The scene is now revealed in closer detail, though
it is very important to remember that John is still having a
vision. Three times (11, 17, 19) he says, 'I saw'. There is no
way in which you can argue for a strictly literal interpretation of what we find here.

The enemy gathers
Start with verse 19's picture of the gathering together of
'the beast and the kings of the earth and their armies . . .
to make war against the rider on the horse and his army'.
What is this gathering together? It appears that it is part
of God's sovereign and mysterious purposes that all the
forces of evil should in a special way and with a peculiar

force be marshalled together at the end of the age. Every-one's true colours will increasingly be revealed, and so that means that the true nature of those who hate God and His people, hate Christ and His church, will be exposed. We must not think of this as a third world war or some sort of nuclear confrontation. Rather think back to those characters in chapter 13, the two beasts, and what they stood for. What is pictured under this symbol of the gathering of Christ's enemies is an intensifying of their activity, especially the exercise of anti-Christian power against the true church and the further spawning of false religions and counterfeit cults. More and more people will be deceived by the devil's lies and deceptions and taken in by his false promises. The whole position of the church and the Christian will become more and more difficult — though, on another subject, this should not have the effect of making us doubt the importance and possibility of revival, and so God's pouring out of His Spirit in exceptional measure upon the church. For we have no idea at all of God's timetable. We may think things have never been so bad before as they are now, and so the end is bound to come any moment. But many have quite genuinely felt that before us, but it was not yet the end, and God intervened again in grace and revival. We just do not know.

However, we should remember that the world in its essential characteristic as hostile to God, His ways, His gospel and His laws, and so hostile to His people, will not change, but rather increase as the end draws nearer. And all this heightening of enemy action will be at its pinnacle when, all of a sudden . . .

The King comes
Look back to verse 11. Back in chapter 4:1, at the commencement of his visions into some of God's mysteries, John remarked that 'There before me was a door standing open in heaven.' He was given a glimpse, then another glimpse, and so on, of 'what must soon take place' (1:1). But now he tells us, 'I saw heaven standing open.' He is given even grander and fuller views than before, and straight away the whole picture is occupied by Christ on the white horse. For that is who the Rider on the white horse is! The Lord Jesus Christ Himself.

Here are all the nations, all the enemies of God, all the
forces of evil rising in increasingly furious rebellion against
Christ, all gathered (symbolically) upon the battlefield of
Armageddon, when the very One against whom they are
fighting appears. And He comes not this time in the
humiliation of Bethlehem or Calvary, but in all His glory.
As we remarked a long way back in our study, the horse
is symbolic of war and white is the colour of victory. Here
comes Christ to win a full and final victory over all His
enemies.

He is called 'Faithful and True'. He is faithful, for He
comes as He has promised His people that He would. The
coming again in glory at the end of the age, according to
the terms of Matthew 24:30–31 and Acts 1:11, is the
great object of our Christian hope, for if He does not come
our hope would be in vain, our trials would be cruel jokes
and our whole lives would come to nothing. But He is
coming. He is called Faithful. And He is called True. There
have been and will continue to be many false Christs and
false prophets before the end comes, but the Lord Jesus
Christ is who He says He is and will perform all that He
has promised.

v. 12. Mention has been made before in the book of
Revelation of Christ's eyes 'like blazing fire' (cf. 1:14).
His look penetrates the darkness and the deepest corner of
wickedness, laying everything and everyone bare. No
pretence or hypocrisy will escape His gaze, once He comes
in judgement. 'There is nothing concealed that will not be
disclosed, or hidden that will not be made known' (Matthew
10:26). 'And on his head are many crowns.' This is so
already, for by His death at Calvary and His glorious
resurrection He overcame sin and destroyed the devil and
his works. The battle of Armageddon is only the climax
of the holy war which the Lord Jesus Christ has been fighting
and winning throughout the ages!

v. 13. The blood in which Christ's robe is dipped in this
vision is not His own shed blood but the spilled blood of
His enemies. This picture is very reminiscent of Isaiah 63
and the picture early on in that chapter of Christ 'robed in
splendour, striding forward in the greatness of His strength',
with His 'garments red, like those of one treading the
winepress'. The Lord Himself says there,

> 'I have trodden the winepress alone;
>> from the nations no one was with me.
> I trampled them in my anger
>> and trod them down in my wrath;
> their blood spattered my garments,
>> and I stained all my clothing'
>>> (Isaiah 63:1—3).

What a glorious Victor our Saviour is! And His name is **'the Word of God'**. He comes from the Father, is the express image of the Father and makes Him known.

v. 14. Once again, His people are with Him (cf. 14:1). His victories are our victories. His people overcome through Him. It is altogether too narrow to take the **'armies of heaven'** as meaning only angels. The reference most certainly is to Christ's people, His saints. Like their Captain they too are riding on white horses and the reference to their dress (cf. 19:8) clinches the matter. It makes us think as well of 1 Corinthians 6:2, that amazing verse which teaches us: 'Do you not know that the saints will judge the world?'

v. 15. For the third time in the book we meet this quote from Psalm 2, that psalm which so magnificently sets forth the kingly authority of the Lord Jesus Christ and the obedience of the nations to Him. This whole verse makes Christ's victory look so easy!

v. 16. What a name — **'King of kings and Lord of lords'**! His is truly 'the name high over all'. The history of the world is littered with kings and lords who have come, been hailed and followed for a season and then have disappeared from view — here today and gone tomorrow, just like everything else that belongs to 'this world'. Men who refuse to bow to the sovereignty of Christ and are concerned ultimately with the glory of man, not least their own, will go the way of all flesh. But now, on the field of battle, someone altogether different appears: the One whose kingdom is an everlasting kingdom and whose divine lordship is from everlasting to everlasting.

The battle ends

Two portions of the chapter remain for us to remark upon: the announcement of the angel (17—18) and the further description of Christ's victory (20—21).

The little section of verses 17—18 symbolizes the complete victory of the Rider on the white horse and the utter, shameful and final defeat of the enemy. This is described most vividly under the symbol of a great supper, though a very different supper from the one back in verse 9! This supper here is a terrifying one, with the birds of the air gorging away in vulture fashion at the flesh of Christ's enemies, from the greatest to the least. The giving of flesh to the birds of the air is a familiar Old Testament picture, expressive of the complete defeat and shameful public subjection and disgrace of the enemies of God, His Christ and His people (cf. Ezekiel 39:4).

So there only remains the capture and destruction of the beast and the false prophet. A number of commentators rightly make the point that we are not to think of these as two real, literal characters who will be destroyed. Rather we need always to keep in mind all that we have learned concerning what they stand for. We dealt with that in our treatment of chapter 13. What is portrayed here, therefore, is the final end to all devilry, anti-Christian persecution, anti-gospel counterfeiting and all the rest of the devil's works. The destruction of Satan himself is reserved for chapter 20.

As we leave this chapter there is a need for self-examination. Where do you belong in this battle? On which side are you? Oh, that we might all be fighting and secure under the banner of the Lord Jesus Christ, the Captain of our salvation — the King of kings and the Lord of lords! At any time, and not least when Armageddon comes, the only security to be found will be in Christ's camp; for all those who have 'received the mark of the beast and worshipped his image' will have been deluded, and will be defeated and destroyed.

18.
A thousand years

Please read Revelation 20

The millennium! Here we are at chapter 20! People have often felt rather apprehensive about this chapter, but there is no need to be. Remember a note we struck in our introduction: the Holy Spirit has been given to lead us into all truth.

As you read Revelation 20, what strikes you most? What is the most often-repeated phrase? Did you notice that 'thousand years' appears in each of the verses from verses 2—7 inclusive? That is six times. People speak of the millennium in connection with this chapter of Scripture, and all that word means is 'a period of one thousand years'. It is quite an ordinary and usual word — not half so threatening as some have tended to make it! So, obviously, central to our understanding of this chapter is a right view of the teaching concerning the thousand years.

1. Satan bound: The view from the earth (1—3)

Once again we are faced with a bewildering array of visions and symbols. First of all John saw 'an angel coming down out of heaven'. This angel held 'the key to the Abyss' — a deep hole or shaft with a lid on it which could be unlocked, locked or locked and sealed. Notice also what else the angel held — a great chain in his hand. So it seems that what he is about to do is this: chain someone up, lock him in the Abyss and then seal it up so that he cannot let himself out or escape. And that is exactly what the angel did! But to whom? The devil (2); the angel overpowered Satan,

rendered him helpless, bound him up and locked him away
for a thousand years.

There is the symbol; but what does it mean? This binding
of Satan takes us back once again to the first coming of
Christ. Have a look at Luke 11:21—22. In Jesus' teaching
there, Satan is the strong man and Christ Himself is the
One stronger than he, who has come to bind him and spoil
his goods. Up until Christ came (cf. 20:3) Satan had blinded
the eyes of the nations and deceived them. By and large
salvation had been limited to the Jews and many of them
had remained unbelieving and hostile to God. But then
Christ did come and things changed — the millennium,
the (symbolic) thousand years, began. The Lord Jesus
Christ triumphed over the devil at the time of the
temptations in the wilderness. He triumphed over the devil
when He cast out the demons who had possessed various
people. He triumphed over the devil as the gospel began
to be preached to Greeks and Samaritans as well as to Jews.
In Colossians 2:15 Paul makes a direct link between Christ's
Calvary work and the binding and spoiling of Satan: 'And
having disarmed the powers and authorities, He made a
public spectacle of them, triumphing over them by the
cross.' If you look up Hebrews 2:14, you will find that it
says much the same concerning Christ's resurrection. And
1 John 3:8 sums it all up: 'The reason the Son of God
appeared was to destroy the devil's work.'

So we should be in a position now where we can begin
to understand chapter 20:3. From the time of Christ's
first coming, Satan has been bound. The symbolic thousand-
year period — the millennium — is the period we are in at
this very moment.

'But,' you say, 'is Satan really bound? Look at all his
activity — all the evil in the world, all the counterfeits of
Christianity, all the lies, delusions and persecutions that
abound. Is he really bound?'

Certainly Satan is mightily active. Already the book
of Revelation has given us a potent testimony on that score.
But it is the strictly limited (even though furious and danger-
ous) activity of the dog on a chain. Or, to take a more
unusual analogy, it is like the famous American gangster,
Al Capone, running Chicago from Chicago Gaol. Plenty of

activity, plenty of damage — but a strict limit to Satan's power and sphere of operation. If the dog were not on the chain, or if old Al Capone were not in the gaol, things would be very different. So with Satan. There is all the difference between being powerful and bound and being powerful and free.

The truth of the gospel has in many nations and many hearts replaced the lie of the devil. The church of God has been planted and established in numerous places. Numberless throngs from among the nations, tribes. peoples and tongues of the world have been drawn to faith in the Lord Jesus Christ. The Bible has been translated into countless languages and dialects. And still the work goes on.

Do not think that the world as such is becoming better and better. Do not imagine that all who hear the gospel believe it and receive it. Do not entertain false hopes that the majority will be on the side of Christ when He appears. The devil is not bound in every sense. But he is a doomed and defeated foe of Christ.

2. Saints alive: The view from heaven (4–6)

If in verses 1–3 we find the millennium viewed from the earthly aspect, in verses 4–6 we find the same period viewed from the heavenly aspect. Again, be clear about the details of what John saw in his vision. He saw thrones — a detail which, in the context of the book of Revelation, places the scene indisputably in heaven. Who were on the thrones? The souls (not the bodies, only the souls) of 'those who **had been beheaded because of their testimony for Jesus and because of the word of God**' and, more broadly, all true believers who '**had not worshipped the beast or his image and had not received his mark on their foreheads or their hands**'.

They had gone through '**the first resurrection**' (5), which is a reference to the immediate glorification of believers after their death (look back and consider again our remarks on 6:9–11). '**They came to life and reigned with Christ.**' The story is told of the famous American evangelist, D. L. Moody, who one day was addressing a company of people.

'One of these fine mornings', he is reported as saying, 'you will read in your newspaper that D. L. Moody is dead. Don't you believe it! On that day I shall be more alive than I have ever been!' We are reminded of that fine statement in the Westminster Confession of Faith concerning the souls of the faithful: 'The bodies of men after their death return to dust and see corruption; but their souls (which neither die nor sleep) having an immortal subsistence, immediately return to God who gave them. The souls of the righteous, being then made perfect in holiness, are received into the highest heavens, where they behold the face of God in light and glory, waiting for the full redemption of their bodies.'

Their condition is 'blessed and holy' (6), and 'the second death' (the ultimate state of eternal death in hell) cannot hurt them. We are back again to the brilliant truth of Romans 8:1: no condemnation for those in Jesus! At the general resurrection at the last day, of course, their souls will be united with their new resurrection bodies and the promise given back in chapter 3:21 will be realized in full!

3. Satan's little season: The final conflict (7–10)

Go back for a moment to the end of verse 3: 'After that [the millennium], he [Satan] must be set free for a short time.' Now come on to verse 7, which begins: 'When the thousand years are over . . .' Then what will happen? Satan will be released from his prison house, bound in the Abyss, and will have a terrible final fling. There will be a period of deception, persecution and fury coming upon the whole world — 'the nations in the four corners of the earth' — when the church will be cruelly persecuted and bitterly oppressed. Described in these final conflict terms in the verses we are looking at is the great battle of Armageddon which we noticed briefly in chapter 16 and studied in detail in chapter 19.

What do we make of 'Gog and Magog'? The expression comes from Ezekiel chapters 38 and 39, a prophecy about the days of a terrible persecution against God's people instigated by Antiochus Epiphanes of Syria. Dr Hendriksen remarks that 'The book of Revelation uses this period of affliction and woe as a symbol of the final attack of Satan and his hordes upon the church' and urges us to consider the fourfold resemblance as follows:

1. The attack of Gog and Magog (Syria under Antiochus) was the last great attack upon the people of God in the Old Testament.
2. The enemy forces were very numerous.
3. The tribulation was terrible though of limited duration.
4. The defeat of the enemy was sudden and complete.

Truly the resemblance is remarkable! We sometimes refer to this period of Armageddon as 'Satan's little season'.

Yet although such appalling might and force will be arrayed against the people of God, just see how the church is described and viewed by God in verse 9 — the symbolism of 'the camp of God's people, the city he loves'! Suddenly — even while the oppression is at its height and it looks as if the true church has finally had it, the Lord Jesus Christ will appear from heaven and the devil will be consumed and destroyed. The great deceiver, who had deceived the wicked into thinking that sin really does pay, that God can be ignored and that victory over the church of God really is possible, is suddenly cast into hell, 'into the lake of burning sulphur' (10) — gone for ever! Christ's triumph is complete. He alone reigns, having put down all His enemies under His feet. The last enemy (death and him who has the power of it, 1 Corinthians 15:25–26) has been punished and destroyed (cf. 14).

And so the scene is finally set for the last judgement.

4. The last judgement (11–15)

The words 'then I saw' indicate the commencement of a new vision. What the apostle John is given here is a remarkably detailed vision of the Day of Judgement, painted in vigorous colours. Here is the day that God has fixed 'when he will judge the world with justice by the man he has appointed' (Acts 17:31). It is a day in which you and I — everyone — will be involved.

Four features of the vision took John's attention.

The throne

John saw 'a great white throne and him who was seated on it'. 'Great' indicates the magnitude of the judgement which is to take place before it and the enormous seriousness of the sentences which will be issuing from it. 'White' is symbolic of the holiness, purity and glory of the One whose throne it is and so carries also the assurance of the absolute justice of the judgements which will proceed from the throne. They will not be partial, or out of favouritism, or in any sense corrupt, but spotless, true and just, and they will be acknowledged as such by all. No one will have any grounds for disputing the Judge's conclusions, whether His condemnations or His acquittals. 'Will not the Judge of all the earth do right?' (Genesis 18:25.)

And who is this Judge, this One seated upon the throne? Some say God Himself. Some say the Lord Jesus Christ, the Second Person of the Godhead. Perhaps the best answer to give is this: it is God Himself who is seated on the throne, but He judges the world through His Son, the Lord Jesus Christ. In this matter, as ever, the Father and the Son are one (John 10:30). But it serves to remind us that the Father has committed authority and judgement to the Son (Matthew 28:18; John 5:22–27) and that how we fare on the judgement day will depend upon our relationship to Christ Himself.

And look at the effect of the Judge's presence and appearance, as verse 11 continues! And people make jokes about the Judgement Day!

The judged

We have seen the Judge, but who are the ones being judged? The passage does not leave us in any doubt, for John saw 'the dead, great and small, standing before the throne' (12). That is to say, everyone who has ever lived, from Adam, who was the first man who ever lived, to the very last man who shall ever live. Cain and his murdered brother Abel will be there, so will Noah along with all those who laughed at him and perished in the flood; all the Old Testament believers and their enemies and persecutors will be there; characters like Judas, Pilate and Herod will be there; so will the apostles of the New Testament and all the evangelical martyrs – indeed all the people of God throughout the centuries. All will be there. No one who has ever lived will be missing.

'**Great and small**' is another reminder that no earthly distinctions that people made for themselves or that others made for them will be valid any longer. The powerful and the insignificant, the famous and the never-heard-of, parents and children, rulers and subjects, rich and poor, pop-stars and fans, heroes and worshippers, professors and illiterates, pastors and their flocks, bosses and their employees, governments and electorates — none will be too high and none will be too low (cf. 6:15; 11:18).

Then notice the beginning of verse 13. The majority who appear will already have been dead for a long time, of course, but still they will be raised for judgement, however they died — whether peacefully in their beds, mangled in a car crash, blown to pieces by terrorists, or even those who went down to a watery grave in the seas. Don't ask me how it will all happen. It is not ours to stage-manage. Only God can perform wonders. Our concern should be to prepare for that day. But while all will be raised for the judgement, all will not be raised to hear the same word from the Judge.

The books

What a telling, sonorous phrase we have in verse 12: '**And books were opened**'! Now these books are symbolic, like so much else in Revelation. We do not need to ask the question: 'What literally are these books?' but rather, 'What do they represent?' And the answer surely cannot be missed: they represent a record of all that has taken place throughout the whole of our lives. '**The dead were judged according to what they had done as recorded in the books**' (12); '**each person was judged according to what he had done**' (13) (cf. 2 Corinthians 5:10). All our internals and all our externals will be taken into account — our actions, our words, our thoughts and our motives, our most secret and intimate habits and desires, the things we have done in the light and the things we have done in the dark, how we have lived, for whom we have lived and our use of our gifts and talents.

Most readers will no doubt be familiar with the long-running programme on British television called *This Is Your*

Life, but it would be very strange and unusual if anyone were exposed or embarrassed on that programme. Everything is jolly, congratulatory and so on. In a sense it is all very unreal and incomplete. But the Judgement Day will not be like that, for when the books are opened, all will be revealed. The value, the character, the true worth, the whole set of every person's life and work will be laid bare.

And if, in the light of this, anyone is inclined to ask, 'Doesn't this mean, then, that after all I can get myself right with God on the basis of my works, leading a good life, and so on?', the answer is 'No!' For **'Another book was opened, which is the book of life'** (12). In chapter 21:27 it is called 'the Lamb's book of life'. In this book are written the names of God's elect — God's own people who have been brought to trust in the Lord Jesus Christ and who have been reconciled to God on the basis not of their own works, their own merit, their own righteousness, their own life, their own death, but on Christ's works, Christ's merit, Christ's righteousness, Christ's life and Christ's death.

All believers, along with everyone else, will have their lives reviewed in intimate detail. We shall see more clearly and appallingly than before what was the weight of our sins and corruptions and backslidings. But we shall also see more clearly and gloriously than ever before the largeness of God's grace in saving us and the perfection of Christ's work covering us and availing for us, to bring us to God. So we shall have nothing to fear at the judgement, for Christ has already been judged in our place, the Just for the unjust.

The sentence
Taking verses 14—15 together, what is the basis of the distinction in sentences proceeding from the throne? It is this: how a man stands in relation to God — and so whether or not a person is 'in Christ', believing in Christ, belonging to Christ. Is your name written in the book of life, or not? Are you trusting in Christ alone, or not? Is your claim to possess the new birth underscored and confirmed by the evidences of the new life, or not? These are not theoretical questions! Eternity hangs upon them — a glorious eternity in heaven or a lost eternity in hell. Jonathan Edwards once

wrote, 'Let it be considered, that if our lives be not a journey to heaven they will be a journey to hell.'

The Lord Jesus Christ teaches very plainly that 'Whoever hears my word and believes him who sent me has eternal life and will not be condemned; he has crossed over from death to life' (John 5:24). But only a moment later He makes it equally plain that some, at the judgement and resurrection, 'will rise to live' and some 'will rise to be condemned' (John 5:29). There is a resurrection to glory, life and joy, and there is a resurrection to eternal punishment (that 'lake of fire . . . the second death', 14).

Think carefully. Think seriously. Think *now* about these things. How do you stand? Where do you stand?

'Whoever believes in the Son has eternal life, but whoever rejects the Son will not see life, for God's wrath remains on him' (John 3:36).

19.
All things new!

Please read Revelation 21

We have had cause to remark before on the different 'feel', the complete change of atmosphere, to be found in moving from one chapter of Revelation to another. And now it happens again! The description of the destructive nature of God's programme is now ended. One by one, we have witnessed the destruction of all His enemies — the beast, the false prophet, seductive Babylon and, just now at the end of chapter 20, the devil himself. All hatred towards God has been removed and what now remains is a most wonderful picture of the positive and glorious results of all Christ's work, the final and complete realization of all God's promises, the long-awaited and magnificent reward of the righteous who are 'more than conquerors through him who loved us' (Romans 8:37).

Chapter 21 really divides into two portions of unequal length. The first section (1–8) revolves around God's statement in verse 5: 'I am making everything new!' The second section (9–27) focuses upon 'the Holy City, Jerusalem, coming down out of heaven from God' (10). The whole vision will then be completed in our next chapter, with the view of 'paradise restored' in chapter 22:1–5.

1. The vision of 'all things new'

'Then I saw' provides the by now familiar words for the beginning of a fresh vision. What did John see?

180

1. He saw 'a new heaven and a new earth' (1)

Pictured here is God's glorious work of the re-creation of the heavens and the earth. At the very beginning of the Bible, in Genesis 1:1, we read the fundamental statement that 'In the beginning God created the heavens and the earth' — the statement of God's original, sovereign work of creation, out of nothing, by the word of His power. Yet it is all going to pass away. The Lord Jesus Christ said so Himself: 'Heaven and earth will pass away' (Mark 13:31).

And Peter tells us that 'In keeping with his promise we are looking forward to a new heaven and a new earth, the home of righteousness' (2 Peter 3:13). Furthermore, the whole business was spoken of way back in the Old Testament — have a look at Psalm 102:25–27 and Isaiah 65:17.

In this vision this is what John saw — the new heaven and the new earth created by God. But the Bible has two words for 'new'. One of them is used for a brand-new creation, like the first creation; but that is not the word found here. Our word means 'new' in the sense of a radically transformed, rejuvenated and renewed heaven and earth. The section of 2 Peter 3, to which we have already referred (cf. 2 Peter 3:10, 12) speaks of the heavens being destroyed by fire and the elements melting in the heat. Such indeed, will be the case, yet this does not mean utter annihilation. Rather (to use John's verb in verse 1b) it is a 'passing away', a burning up of everything that had to do with sin and the curse. That will include all the foul things mentioned in verse 8, as well as features like weeds, thorns and thistles which represent God's curse upon nature, and things like wars, disease, dangers, earthquakes and volcanoes. Nothing will be left to harm or to destroy. Nothing will remain that belongs to iniquity or unrighteousness. The new heaven and the new earth will be a perfect abode for God and His people. Surely Ephesians 1:10 must come in here: all things in heaven and earth united in the Lord Jesus Christ, who will be Head over all in the new creation.

As an extra detail, the statement **'and there was no longer any sea'** underscores this. The sea stands as the emblem of roaring unrest and raging conflict — all gone! Old things, former things, will have passed away. All things will have become new!

2. John saw the new Jerusalem (2)

We shall reserve a close treatment of this for when we come
to verses 9—11. For now, notice just one crucial thing.
Look very carefully at verse 2. Stare at it, in case there
is something there you have always missed before. Do you
see the clear identity in the vision between 'the Holy City,
the new Jerusalem' and the '**bride beautifully dressed for
her husband**'? So? Precisely this: the city is the bride, and
the bride is the city. We know who the bride is from chapter
19:7—8: the true church of Christ, born of God by His Holy
Spirit. This ties in exactly with the reference to the city
'**coming down out of heaven from God**'. So the new
Jerusalem cannot be a literal city. It is the same as the
bride. It is the church triumphant in glory being presented
here to her Husband, the Lord Jesus Christ, at the marriage
supper of the Lamb. Remember that back in chapter 20:9
God's people were described as 'the city he loves', and the
Old Testament pictures the church under the symbolism
of the city as well (for example, Psalm 48:1—2, 12—13;
Isaiah 26:1). Another lovely instance of the unity of
Scripture!

*3. John's attention was focused upon God's fellowship with
His people* (3—4)

What would you say was the 'motto' of God's covenant with
His people? 'I will be their God and they will be my people'
(Jeremiah 31:33). Now during the Old Testament period,
God dwelt among His own people Israel. He dwelt in the
temple, and particularly in the most holy place of the temple,
reigning over His people, protecting them from their enemies,
forgiving their sins, and so on. But to a large extent this
was an external relationship, whereas through the Lord Jesus
Christ — through His incarnation, death and resurrection
and the gift of the Holy Spirit — God now dwells among
His people in a different way. He dwells in our hearts and
lives. He has written His laws upon our minds and hearts.
Our very bodies are temples of His Holy Spirit. Christ dwells
in our hearts by faith. He reigns over us from within.

But still there are imperfections in God's fellowship with
His people — imperfections, let us quickly say, arising only
upon His people's part, as sin continues to rear its ugly head

in our lives, seeking to draw us away from God. But in the days of the new heaven and new earth, all this will be changed. God will truly and perfectly live with His people. Feast upon the glorious details in verses 3—4. As ever, the heavenly glories in themselves we cannot yet imagine or comprehend, so they are described for us here by way of comparison with present things: no more tears; no more death; no more mourning or crying or pain. Isaac Watts sums it up:

> Sin, my worst enemy before,
> Shall vex my eyes and ears no more;
> My inward foes shall all be slain,
> Nor Satan break my peace again.
>
> Then shall I see, and hear, and know
> All I desired or wished below;
> And every power find sweet employ
> In that eternal world of joy.

Again, the old order of things has passed away — all things have become new!

But tell me: have you ever had that feeling that things sound too good to be true? And does there strike you something almost unbelievable about what we are considering now? Perhaps for that very reason God Himself immediately adds three clear confirmations which we can pick out briefly here: God's statement (5), God's name (6a) and God's reminders (6b—8).

His statement is this: 'These words are trustworthy and true.' That says all that we need to hear in order to be absolutely assured that all God says about the new heaven and the new earth, His people as Christ's bride and the intimacy of His fellowship with His people is not insurance policy stuff or pie-in-the-sky. It is real. It is true. 'In his great mercy he has given us new birth into a living hope' (1 Peter 1:3) and that hope will never prove a disappointment or a delusion.

His name is 'the Alpha and the Omega, the Beginning and the End'. The first of these titles has already appeared in chapter 1:18 and they are both to appear again, along with

'the First and the Last', in chapter 22:13. We are reminded
also of Isaiah 46:10: 'I make known the end from the
beginning, from ancient times, what is still to come. I say:
My purpose will stand, and I will do all that I please.' And
all of this is against the mighty backcloth of God's everlastingness: 'From everlasting to everlasting you are God'
(Psalm 90:2).

In this character God says in our verse, 'It is done'. From
the very beginning God made all things with a view to the
end — the 'alpha' must inevitably lead to the 'omega'. He
controls everything in such a way that all His counsel is
accomplished, all His designs fulfilled, all His promises
performed and all His ends are reached.

His reminders are twofold. Salvation and adoption are
the free gift of God's grace — living water for thirsty souls
(6b–7). But there is always the other side of the coin.
The second death (everlasting desolation and anguish and
the dreadful experience of the wrath of God without end)
is all that awaits those who reject the gracious invitation
'to drink without cost from the spring of the water of life'.
But if you compare verse 8 with 1 Corinthians 6:9–11,
what a reminder of the life-changing power of the gospel —
'the power of God for the salvation of everyone who
believes'! (Romans 1:16.)

2. The vision of 'the Holy City'

And so we come to one of the loveliest, most mouth-watering
portions of the Bible. We saw the key to its interpretation
back in verse 2: the city is the bride, and the bride is the
city. That means that what we have in verses 9–27 is not
primarily a picture of heaven, though it has everything to
do with the life of heaven, but primarily a picture of the
glorified church gathered together to God. The spotlight
falls upon four features.

The glory of the church (9–11, 18–21)
John received an invitation from 'one of the seven angels
who had the seven bowls full of the seven last plagues', and
what an invitation it was! 'Come, I will show you the bride,

the wife of the Lamb.' Presumably this is the same angel as the one who showed John the great prostitute (17:1). 'The use of the same angel to introduce both visions thus presents a striking contrast between the doom of the harlot city and the glory of the holy city.'[34]

Then it was that, 'carried . . . away in the Spirit to a mountain great and high', John saw not a bride, but a city — hence our identification of the one with the other. It must be so. And the thing that struck John most impressively about this city 'coming down out of heaven from God' is that 'it shone with the glory of God'. (In this connection, notice from verses 18 and 21 that 'the (street of the) city was of pure gold'.) The glory of the church is what made its mark upon the apostle! But how can you set that forth in ordinary human language?

But stop! Wait a minute! Think back. John has faced a similar problem before. When given the vision of the glory of God in chapter 4, what means did he employ then to set that glory forth? He used the language of precious stones. So now that he needs to speak of the church shining with the glory of God, it would not be surprising to find him resorting to that same language again. And that is exactly what he does!

First he goes for the jasper: 'Its brilliance was like that of a very precious jewel, like a jasper, clear as crystal.' This very stone was mentioned in chapter 4:3 to describe the appearance of God. The jasper, like our diamond, is absolutely clear, transparent, brilliantly bright. And so the meaning becomes clear as this applies to the church. The glory of God is at last imparted to the glorified church and thoroughly reflected in her. All God's infinite perfections and virtues, all His knowledge and grace and righteousness and love and holiness and wisdom and goodness are reflected in the church. The church is adorned with the glory of God, radiated with it, filled with it — aglow with it!

Do you remember Psalm 29:2, with its call to 'worship the Lord in the splendour [beauty, AV] of his holiness'? Well, that beauty of that holiness of God is further reflected in His church by means of the picture of the many precious stones in verses 18–21. What a sight for John's eyes! What a glorious display of exquisite colour — reds (like the carnelian), greens (emerald and beryl), flesh colour (sardonyx), yellow and gold (chrysolite, topaz, chrysoprase), the blue of the sapphire, the violet of the jacinth, the purple of the amethyst and, once more, the brilliant diamond-like clarity of the jasper. Not to mention the pearls and the pure gold of verse 21!

This should help us to understand something of the depth of the apostle John's statement elsewhere: 'We shall see him as he is' (1 John 3:2), or what Paul means when he speaks of our being 'filled to the measure of all the fulness of God' (Ephesians 3:19). This is what Christ died for (Ephesians 5:27)! This is the ultimate goal of our election (Ephesians 1:4)!

The security of the church (12–14, 17–18, 21)
Here the symbol of the church as the city is very much to the fore. Notice the mention, in turn, of the city wall, the gates and the foundations.

The city wall is described as great and high (12), 144 cubits (c. 220 feet) thick or high (17), and made of jasper (18). There are not many cities that have them these days, and whenever we hear of 'new towns' being built, a city wall is not part of the planning. But if you live in York, as I do, you can still see plenty of the old city wall in evidence, and the same is true of some other cities in England.

What is the purpose of a city wall? It is for security and protection; it keeps the enemy out and looks after the city-dwellers inside. Now while in glory there will be no evil for us to be protected from (for the reason given later in verse 27) and no evil one still around to attack the church, it still stands as a most delightful and comforting picture of the security and protection that are the gift and privilege of the church of God.

Psalms 91:4 and 61:2 present the same truth under different pictures — the wings of refuge and the high rock. And Psalm 125:1–2, which we noted earlier in the book, is a matchless testimony to this truth also. But remember that one of the themes running through Revelation is that even now the church of God is secured. Though attacked and assaulted from outside and tossed to and fro from inside, the true church cannot be destroyed. In essence, the church

right now is glorious, and the church right now is secure!
That is why Toplady could write:

> Yes, I to the end shall endure
> As sure as the earnest is given;
> More happy, but not more secure,
> The glorified spirits in heaven.

Our God is glorious, loving and protecting!

The gates numbered twelve in all (three on the east,
three on the north, three on the south and three on the
west, 13). Each gate was made of a single pearl, and they
had 'the names of the twelve tribes of Israel' written upon
them. Take these gates with the foundations.

The foundations also numbered twelve, and upon them
were written 'the names of the twelve apostles of the Lamb'
(14), so including John's own name!

Together, what do the gates and foundations, with their
respective names on them, signify? Surely this: all the elect
of God are safely gathered in. The city, in other words, is
complete and finished. No one is missing who should be
there. Christ has not lost a single one of all those whom
the Father gave Him (John 6:39–40; 10:28). The names
of the twelve tribes of Israel and the names of the twelve
apostles of the Lamb represent the victorious conclusion
of the plan of redemption. We shall keep some lovely
company in glory – all God's people from Old Testament
days, New Testament days and all the days since then!

It is natural to make a comparison with Isaiah 60:18,
where it is said of Zion (the church), 'You will call your
walls Salvation and your gates Praise.' It is in His gift of
salvation that God is most largely glorified and this is His
people's supreme subject when they praise Him. Remember
the song of the redeemed back in chapter 7:10.

The angels at the gates (12) are the angels who have
served God in the work of gathering in the citizens of
heaven (Mark 13:27).

The intimacy of the church's fellowship with God (15–17)
How does this arise from these verses? Notice very carefully
what happens. John is told by the angel to measure the

city — and even the measuring rod is made of gold! What do
you observe? The city is as long as it is wide as it is high
(16) — 12,000 stadia (1,400 miles) in each case. Of course,
all these figures and measurements in chapter 21 are symbolic! But what do you call something with this shape and
equality of measurement? A perfect cube.

Now then: here is something to test your Bible knowledge.
What else was a perfect cube? The answer is the Holy of
Holies in the tabernacle and then in the temple, where the
high priest went only once a year (1 Kings 6:20). So the
thought is a very sweet one. The church has become the
perfect dwelling place of God (cf. 3). Just as in that special
and particular sense God dwelt in the most holy place, so
here is God dwelling in the very midst of His people, so
that the fellowship and communion we shall enjoy with
Him will be perfect and intimate. God Himself will be the
very life of heaven.

James Renwick was one of the Scottish Covenanters put
to death in the seventeenth century for his unswerving
testimony to the Saviour, the Head of the church. As he
awaited the harsh order to climb the 'death ladder' to the
gallows, he said, 'I shall soon be above these clouds; then
I shall enjoy Thee and glorify Thee without interruption
or intermission for ever.'[35]

The life of the church (22–27)
What will life in heaven be like? What shall we do? How
shall we be? These closing verses of the chapter show us a
life of worship, activity and purity.

It will be *a life of worship* (22–23). There will be no
need to 'go to church' as a distinctive activity in a particular
place. Merely to be in the city, just to belong to God's
people, will be to be with Him. That is why we find in
verse 22 that John did not see a temple in the city: **'For the
Lord God Almighty and the Lamb are its temple.'**

The radiancy, majesty and glory of 'the Lord God
Almighty and the Lamb', furthermore, will pervade every
nook and cranny of the place. Hence verse 23: no sun or
moon are needed to brighten things up, **'for the glory of
God gives its light, and the Lamb is its lamp'**. Even the
closest walk with God now cannot compare with the joy

and intimacy of being in God's presence in glory. The apostle Paul remarks rightly that

> 'No eye has seen,
>   no ear has heard,
> no mind has conceived
>   what God has prepared for those who love him'
>   (1 Corinthians 2:9)

and the hymn-writer Bernard of Cluny chimes in in agreement:

> I know not, oh, I know not,
> What joys are waiting there,
> What radiancy of glory,
> What bliss beyond compare!

It will be *a life of activity* (24—26). We shall not be lolling about on settees, but serving God in a constant and unwearied activity. Isaiah 60:11 provides the Old Testament background here — the thought cannot be that the 'human' glory or honour of nations and kings can contribute to the glory and splendour of heaven, for the glory of heaven will be God's glory alone. But just as Isaiah's prophecy 'spoke of the day when the brightness of God's presence in Jerusalem would attract the homage of Gentile nations and kings . . . it is appropriate for John to apply this prophecy to the eternal state, because the redeemed are drawn from all the nations of the earth'.[36] All in heaven will do homage to the Lord God. And there will be no dark nights with shut gates for fear of the enemy.

And it will be *a life of purity* (27). There will be no more sin to separate us from God, disqualify us from entering His presence or hinder our fellowship with Him. All the results and practices of sin will have gone. They will be entirely absent. The elect — 'those whose names are written in the Lamb's book of life' — will be holy, through and through.

Reviewing this chapter 21, then, we are thrilled with the picture it gives us of all that God will do and the life of the glorified church of God. But language cannot contain it all. Even this chapter adds up only to a glimpse. When we arrive in heaven, we shall have to confess the same thing that the Queen of Sheba admitted to King Solomon after she had been taken on a conducted tour of his kingdom and had observed his wisdom at first hand: 'Not even half was told me; in wisdom and wealth you have far exceeded the report I heard' (1 Kings 10:7).

This is beautifully captured in a hymn by Elizabeth Mills, who herself died in her twenties. It forms a fitting conclusion to our study of this chapter.

> We speak of the realms of the blest,
> That country so bright and so fair;
> And oft are its glories confessed —
> But what must it be to be there?
>
> We speak of its pavements of gold,
> Its walls decked with jewels so rare;
> Its wonders and beauties untold —
> But what must it be to be there?
>
> We speak of its freedom from sin,
> From sorrow, temptation and care
> From trials without and within —
> But what must it be to be there?
>
> We speak of its service of love,
> The robes which the glorified wear;
> The church of the first-born above —
> But what must it be to be there?
>
> Do thou, Lord, midst pleasure and woe,
> For heaven our spirits prepare;
> And shortly we also shall know
> And feel what it is to be there.

20.
Paradise restored

Please read Revelation 22:1—5

There is a beautiful and amazing unity and symmetry which runs all the way through the Bible and which links together even the first two chapters of Genesis and the last two chapters of Revelation. We cannot miss this as we come now to the beginning of chapter 22 — the beginning of the final chapter of the Word of God. The setting that God created for Adam and Eve, the first human beings whom He created, was 'a garden in the East, in Eden'. In that garden were 'trees that were pleasing to the eye and good for food', and 'In the middle of the garden were the tree of life and the tree of the knowledge of good and evil.' The garden was watered by a river which divided into four headstreams. All this is recorded in Genesis 2:8—10.

Now in Revelation 22 — as the vision of the church of God, the bride of Christ, under the symbol of 'the Holy City, the new Jerusalem, coming down out of heaven from God', continues — we find that a symbolic picture of a garden is, as it were, superimposed upon the picture of the city. But do not be confused! We are still dealing with symbols which add up to a description of the blessedness of the life of the glorified church with Christ in heaven.

The river in paradise (1—2)

The first thing John was shown by the angel was 'the river of the water of life'. There are several things to notice about it.
1. *Its fountainhead:* 'flowing from [out of] the throne of God and of the Lamb';

2. *Its quality:* 'as clear as crystal';

3. *Its position:* central, flowing '**down the middle of the great street of the city**' (in other words, through the very heart of the glorified church).

We are reminded of the language of Psalm 46:4: 'There is a river whose streams make glad the city of God, the holy place where the Most High dwells.'

Taking all these details together, what do they signify? They speak of the gloriously satisfying and God-given life of the church of God in glory. 'Water' and 'the water of life' again and again in the Bible stand for refreshment and satisfaction, and the enriching blessings of free grace salvation (cf. 17). Again, they occur in connection with the Holy Spirit whom Christ gives to His people and who realizes to us and in us all the blessings which Christ has obtained for His people (John 7:37–39). All Christ's blessings flow constantly into the church and so into believers through the One who is the Spirit of Christ, of life, adoption, truth, wisdom, holiness and power; and fulness of blessing, enlargement of blessing, will be the church's portion in glory.

The 'from the throne' is important. God Himself is the ultimate fountain. Every need will be supplied. We shall lack nothing.

The tree in paradise (2)

We recalled earlier that in the middle of the Garden of Eden were two trees (Genesis 2:9). The first of those was 'the tree of life', and that tree had a double significance. In the first place, the tree and its fruit were life-sustaining. They gave Adam and Eve certain necessities of their physical existence. But more than that, in the second place, it was the tree of life in a deeper sense, for life is far more than physical existence. It implied the favour and fellowship of God, it spoke of God dwelling in the midst of His people there in the garden, communing with them whom He had made. Now if we bear all this in mind it will help us with our present verse and paragraph of Revelation.

What does the tree of life in verse 2 symbolize (cf. 2:7)?

First and foremost, it signifies the perfect life of heavenly fellowship with God which all believers will enjoy — the full, heavenly reality of His love, favour and presence. But, secondly, it stresses the eternal reality of this life and fellowship. It will, quite literally, never end!

Notice that this tree of life stands on each side of the river (symbolic again — so don't go away and try to draw it!). It is as if it were a whole park, drawing its life from the waters of the river, which (as we have already seen) proceeds from the very throne of God — the God who, eternally, has life in Himself. And the fruit of the tree is in continual profusion, cropping month by month. All of this underscores the eternal delights of heaven.

The comment concerning **'the leaves of the tree [being] for the healing of the nations'** is a way of saying something we have already learned: no sickness, sin or misery of any kind can ever enter into the city of God or afflict the saved ones. Everything will be life-giving, health-giving and designed to promote the enjoyment of life with God for that 'great multitude that no one could count, from every nation, tribe, people and language'.

The freedom in paradise (3)

The second tree mentioned in Genesis 2 was 'the tree of the knowledge of good and evil', and we know the rest of the story. It was the one tree in the whole of the garden from which God forbade Adam and Eve to eat. God was absolutely straight with them: 'When you eat of it you will surely die' (Genesis 2:17). But they disobeyed God, they sinned against Him and so they came under His death sentence, His judgement and His curse. Genesis 3 records the details.

The curse speaks of God's wrath against sin and His condemnation of the sinner. But the glory of the gospel is that Christ has become a curse for us (Galatians 3:13). As a result, we shall find fully in glory what we know even now by foretaste, that the great excellency of our salvation will be set forth in the fact that **'No longer will there be any curse.'** There will be no serpent, no devil there; no trees bringing curse, no sin there; no temptation, nothing that defiles there. God will have made all things new. 'The throne of God and of the Lamb will be in the city, and his servants will serve him.'

Once that throne was a throne of judgement before which we could not stand. We were under the curse of God. Now, since the Lamb 'interposed His precious blood' for us (as one hymn-writer puts it), it has become for us the throne of grace. What a difference!

The happiness in paradise (4—5)

Yet again it is a case of the foretaste now and the fulness still to come. In what will our happiness chiefly consist?

We shall see his face (4)
With this, compare Psalm 17:15 and Isaiah 33:17. God will be there revealed in the face of His Son, the Lord Jesus Christ, as we have never seen Him before — He who is 'altogether lovely' and 'outstanding among ten thousand'.

His name will be upon our foreheads (4)
This stands for God acknowledging us to be His own. The only other alternative, which we read of back in chapter 13:16, is the mark of the beast. But all those who bore that mark will have gone to the same place as their owner, whose mark it was (19:20; 20:10).

We shall have direct knowledge of God (5)
There will be no more partial views, no more need for the assistance of lamps or even the sun. 'The Lord God will give them light' — we shall know God in the highest, fullest most direct sense possible.

We shall reign for ever and ever (5)
We shall not have any 'subjects' as such, for all Christ's enemies will have long been removed. Rather it gathers up a thought which has been there throughout the book — the blessed and exalted condition of the children of God. As those famous lines have it:

> High is the rank we now possess,
> But higher we shall rise,

for right at the beginning we rejoiced that Christ 'has made us to be a kingdom' (1:16). We shall share in Christ's royalty and we shall live like kings. And we shall be like this for ever and ever!

21.
The end of the Bible

Please read Revelation 22:6—21

Here we are at the end of the book of Revelation. Inevitably this takes on a special importance because it is not just the end of a Bible book, but the end of the whole Bible. Here is God's last word.

Some have suggested that all we have in these verses is a sort of rag-bag or epilogue, an untidy collection of random thoughts and jottings to round things off. It is as if the apostle John had a number of loose ends left over from the visions he had received, and so he threw them into the air, let them fall down and chapter 22:6—21 is the result, so they say. On this view there is no shape to the verses and no theme running through them. But I reject this absolutely. The God-breathed order that belongs to all of Scripture is found here also. The central theme is the sure and certain coming again of the Lord Jesus Christ — the second coming. We can pick out five things in this final section of our exposition.

A welcome reminder (6)

The emphasis here is upon certainty. The angel's words to John, 'These words are trustworthy and true', are set in a wide context. They refer to all that is contained in the book of Revelation, and refer ultimately to all that is written in the whole of Scripture. We shall develop this when we come to verses 18—19. For now, think of it with special reference to Revelation. We have read many strange things, many amazing things, many delightful things and many terrible things in this book. But one thing is sure: everything we have read is true — all the messages of salvation, all the warnings of judgement, all the statements about history! 'Trustworthy and true' are two great words that characterize everything about God, and so everything about God's Word.

This is underscored as the angel continues speaking. The phrase 'the Lord, the God of the spirits of the prophets' (with which compare 19:10) 'means that God illuminates the spirits of the prophets by the inspiration of the Holy Spirit'.[37] So all the things that the angel has declared from God 'must soon take place'. There is no doubting, no uncertainty, no maybe. The faithful will not be disappointed and the wicked will not be overlooked.

A promised event (7–16, 20)

The assurance of Christ's return is here dwelt upon more fully. Christ's own statement, 'I am coming soon!' (7, 12, 20) is the key one. That alone tells us that Christ's coming will be *personal* ('*I* am coming'), *certain* ('I *am coming*') and *ever near* ('I am coming *soon*'). It does not matter what the scoffers say or however passionately men seek to deny this. It is a plain fact — Christ is coming soon. A great chapter of Scripture upon this is 2 Peter 3. Study it carefully, along with Acts 1:11.

Let us follow these verses through.

v. 7. As we have just noticed, the angel quotes Christ's words. The second part of the verse reminds us of chapter 1:3, and the fact that our study of the Word of God and our embracing and increasing understanding of all the doctrines of the Word should lead us to greater obedience and holiness. To say, 'I read the Bible' is not enough. Do you 'do' the Bible?

vv. 8–9. John made the mistake of worshipping the angel. But the angel would not have it, and directed that his homage and worship be directed to God alone. The best of men are but servants at the best, and unprofitable ones at that. And as for the angels, they are not to be worshipped. They

are themselves among those who worship God, and one
of their main tasks which they perform gladly, willingly
and obediently is that of being 'ministering spirits sent
to serve those who will inherit salvation' (Hebrews 1:14).
What vital service this angel who spoke to John rendered!

v. 10. The gospel of God is to be published. The Word of
God is to be proclaimed. There is to be no holding back,
no being ashamed, no watering down, no sealing up. As
the time of Christ's return draws closer, and as the end
of all things is ever nearer at hand, what is the church
doing? What is our task? What is our employment? We
are to be servants, preachers, evangelists, testifiers, warners,
watchers. These are days for being alert and days for being
at work.

v. 11. What does this strange verse mean? On the surface
verse 11a looks like a positive encouragement to the wicked
and godless to continue in their own way. But 'encouragement' would be the wrong word. Nowhere does the Bible
encourage the unbeliever to be an unbeliever, the godless
to continue to be godless or the hell-bound to press on
being hell-bound. On the contrary, the call to the Christless is

> 'Seek the Lord while he may be found;
>   call on him while he is near.
> Let the wicked forsake his way
>   and the evil man his thoughts.
> Let him turn to the Lord, and he will have mercy on
>   him,
>   and to our God, for he will freely pardon'
>   (Isaiah 55:6—7).

But there is an irony in our verse. Although the godless
and the rebellious are to be pleaded with, some will become
increasingly hardened and, the more of the gospel that they
hear, the more summonses to repentance and faith that they
receive, the more warning shots that are fired across their
bows, the more will it all become to them 'the smell of
death' rather than 'the fragrance of life' (2 Corinthians
2:16). And the result will be that those who do wrong
will continue to do wrong, and those who are vile *will*

continue to be vile. Their ways and their hearts will become set firm, as if in concrete. They will not change.

But let the righteous be sure to press on in the way of Christ, cleaving to the Lord, holding firmly to the Word, contending earnestly for the faith and pursuing that holiness without which no one will see the Lord. The doctrine of Christ's second coming has a very powerful incentive for the Christian; it is like dynamite!

vv. 12—15. Christ's words that He is coming soon are repeated. Then He speaks of His 'reward': **'My reward is with me, and I will give to everyone according to what he has done.'** We have seen so clearly throughout the book that Christ brings rewards and punishments — rewards to the righteous and punishments to the wicked. The reward to the righteous, which as with all Christ's rewards is a reward of grace, is set forth in verse 14: the glories of salvation, sanctification and eternal security described in the by now very familiar language of the washed robes, access to the tree of life and citizenship of heaven.

The reward to the unrighteous is set forth in verse 15, beginning with the terrible word **'outside'**. We cannot help thinking back to Noah's day — how when Noah and his family, saved by grace, had gone into the ark, it is recorded that 'The Lord shut him in' (Genesis 7:16). Everyone else was outside and perished in the flood. So it is with those who refuse to enter the kingdom of Christ. The awful characterizations of the wicked in verse 15 speak for themselves, but be sure not to miss the mention of **'magic arts'**. That is a needful word to our generation, so taken up as it is with interest in every occult and devilish practice imaginable.

Who is it who declares all this? It is the Lord Jesus Christ, magnificently described in verse 13: **'I am the Alpha and the Omega, the First and the Last, the Beginning and the End,'** He who has divine authority to save and destroy, for Christ is God. Isaac Watts wrote,

> Before Jehovah's awful throne,
> Ye nations, bow with sacred joy;
> Know that the Lord is God alone,
> He can create, and He destroy.

v. 16. Christ addressed John, but (as the NIV margin informs
us), the 'you' is plural, reminding us again that Christ is
addressing His church, His people. Revelation is timeless,
as we have insisted all along. It is God's Word for all His
people at all times. And just look at the description of the
Lord Jesus Christ here. He says, '**I am the Root and the
Offspring of David.**' The title 'the Root of David' is one
we met in chapter 5:5 and 'Offspring' draws out the meaning all the more plainly. As we saw when commenting
upon that earlier verse, Christ is the promised Messiah,
God's own Son, He is the royal King to whom is given
all power and authority in heaven and earth. He is our
divine and human Saviour.

And do you remember Christ's promise to the believers
at Thyatira (2:28), that He would give them the morning
star? Now He says, '**I am . . . the bright Morning Star.**'
The Old Testament background for the phrase is Numbers
24:17 (cf. 2 Peter 1:19). The point is this: Christ Himself
is coming, and that coming heralds the dawn of everlasting
day when He will give Himself to His people and share
His glory with them in a way which at present is utterly
beyond our imagination.

A gracious invitation (17, 20)

Do you like receiving invitations? This verse contains an
invitation which is in a class of its own. It is an invitation
to those who are thirsty for God, thirsty for the Lord Jesus
Christ, thirsty for salvation, thirsty for heaven.

The opening of the verse finds the Holy Spirit and the
bride (the true church of Christ) uttering a unanimous
'Come!' The more we contemplate the return of Christ,
seeing Christ, being with Christ, reigning with Christ, the
more our desire for it should be increased and our longings
quickened. We might even say, the faster our hearts should
beat! Although the date and time of the Lord's return is
fixed, so that nothing can hurry it and nothing can delay
it, it is still an appropriate subject for the believer to take
up in prayer. When did you last pray, '**Come, Lord Jesus**'?
(20).

Dr Hoeksema remarks attractively: 'This must needs be the spontaneous response of the bride. For the bride receives a picture of the glory of the Bridegroom and of the time when she shall always be with Him. She is conscious all the more, through the prophecy of this book, of her present misery, of her tribulation which she does and must suffer in the midst of the world. She is conscious of her present separation. She is conscious of her sinfulness. And when, through the words of the book of this prophecy, she looks at the glory which shall be revealed to her, she calls out, under the influence of the Spirit of the Bridegroom, "Come; yea come, Lord Jesus!"'

And the second coming of Christ is not only to be prayed for and longed for by the church of Christ. It is also to be preached, so that he 'who hears' will also be caused to cry, '**Come**'. The prospect here is a wonderful one. The gospel is to be preached freely to all who will hear: '**Whoever is thirsty, let him come.**' For all that we have rightly and wonderfully seen in the book of Revelation about God's decree of election and the names that have been written in the Lamb's book of life from before the foundation of the world in no sense removes the necessity, urgency and appropriateness of the free offer of the gospel. '**The free gift of the water of life**' — the Lord Jesus Christ who came into the world to save sinners — is to be offered and preached to all, for it is not ours to know who will receive the gift and who will not. It is ours to preach and plead, in all the enabling power of the Spirit of God. It is God's alone to convict and save.

'For the wages of sin is death, but the gift of God is eternal life in Christ Jesus our Lord' (Romans 6:23). What is your response to Christ's invitation? RSVP!

A fence around the Scriptures (18—19)

What serious verses these are! Christ Himself warns all who hear '**the words of the prophecy of this book**' that they are not to tamper with them in any way, whether by adding anything to them or taking any words away from them. The book of Revelation is to be received, believed and

studied as it stands. Critical scholars who desire to chop
bits out or rearrange the order — hands off! Unbelievers
who find certain parts (or the whole lot) unpalatable and
reject it — beware!

The warning is made all the more serious by the dire
consequences threatened to those who disobey Christ's
order: **'If anyone adds anything . . . God will add to him
the plagues described in this book.'** Such people reveal
by their attitudes and actions that they are not captive
to the Word of God or under the lordship of Christ, and
so have no part in Him. If 'preachers', they are false preachers; if 'believers', they are false believers; if 'professors',
they are false professors. Not Christ and glory, but the
devil and the lake of fire, will be theirs.

**'And if anyone takes words away . . . God will take away
from him his share in the tree of life and in the holy city,
which are described in this book.'** This does not mean that
genuine believers will lose their salvation. That would be to
go against everything that the Word of God (and, not least,
Revelation itself) teaches. Rather it refers to those who
act and speak as though they had a part in Christ and
salvation, whereas really they do not belong to God at
all, and corrupt and distort the very Word of God they
claim to study, teach and follow. It will be manifested
at the last day just who are His and who are not — even
though they persuaded themselves and the church that
they were! In Wilson's fine phrase, such a person 'would
lose what he seemed to have by profession, though as such
an act would prove, not by possession!'

But before we leave these solemn verses we must remark
that they have a wider application. Coming, as they do,
right at the end of the Bible, they provide a fence around
the Scriptures as a whole. I grant that the immediate context of Christ's statement and warning is, as we have just
seen, the book of Revelation itself (**'this book'**). I grant
too, of course, that at the time Revelation was written
what we call 'the Bible' (the sixty-six books of the 'canon'
from Genesis to Revelation) was not in its final shape and
order, though it had all been written. But still, there is an
important sense in which verses 18—19 apply to the whole
of the Bible.

For the Scriptures as a whole, from Genesis 1:1—
Revelation 22:21, comprise the God-breathed Word. Just
as Deuteronomy 4:2 shows us the fence God set around
the Law, and Malachi 4:4 the fence God set around the
whole of the Old Testament, so our present verses declare
the fence which God has set, in a most solemn manner,
around the whole of the New Testament and so around the
whole of the Bible, assuring us that the Bible is a book of
the most sacred nature, divine authority and peculiar care
of God. The Bible is God's last Word, God's final Word.
In the title of one of Dr Packer's books on Scripture, *God
has Spoken.*[38]

So here is a warning to all comers that the Bible as a
whole, the Bible in its entirety, is not to be tampered or
interfered with. Nothing is to be added, for there is nothing
missing that God meant should be there. Nothing is to be
taken away, for there is nothing there upon which God has
changed His mind, which is no longer true, or which has
worn out with the passage of time and become redundant.

So, whether it is Roman Catholics, who add the
Apocrypha (a collection of fourteen Jewish books written
between the close of the Old Testament period and the
beginning of the New) and a whole host of their own human
ideas and traditions like purgatory, prayers for the dead,
the perpetual virginity and the heavenly 'assumption' of
Mary, the infallibility of the pope and so on; or whether
it is the cults, who add their own books and writings and
place them alongside the Scriptures, such as the Mormons,
with *The Book of Mormon, Doctrines and Covenants* and
The Pearl of Great Price, or the Christian Scientists with
Mary Baker Eddy's *Science and Health*; or whether it is
the charismatics who urge that God makes available 'new
truths' and 'fresh revelations' by means of prophecy, tongues
and visions — *nothing is to be added to Scripture.*

And whether it is the argument which says, 'Science has
disproved and discredited the opening chapters of Genesis,
so they'll have to go,' or the whole attitude which urges
that the Bible is all right on (some) doctrinal matters but
has nothing to say on anything else; or whether it is unbelieving archbishops, bishops and other church leaders
who deny vital truths like the virgin birth, literal physical

resurrection and personal and visible second coming of the Lord Jesus Christ, the reality of heaven and hell and all supernaturalism; or whether it is that liberal attitude to Scripture which says that God's rules for marriage, family life and the sanctity of life no longer apply, sexual perversion condemned in Scripture is no longer sexual perversion, the church following God's rules for its life and government is no longer necessary, and any method goes in evangelism — *nothing is to be taken away from Scripture.*

We need to learn again and proclaim afresh the *finality* of Scripture (God has said all that He has to say by way of actual revelation, though, of course, it is the task of the preacher to expound the Word of God vitally and relevantly), and the *sufficiency* of Scripture (we need nothing more, for what God has given us in His Word is all-sufficient as His infallible, inerrant and faultless revelation to us of Himself). It is a sufficiency, argues Paul to Timothy in 2 Timothy 3:14–17, which governs all that is necessary for making people 'wise for salvation through faith in Christ Jesus', showing us what to believe and instructing us how to live.

The last word: grace (21)

The book of Revelation, and indeed the whole Bible, could hardly end in any other way. From first to last — all is of grace! Grace chose us. Grace saved us. Grace keeps us. Grace will present us faultless in glory.

This is expressed in a fine hymn which bears the names of both Philip Doddridge and Augustus Montague Toplady.

> Grace, 'tis a charming sound,
> Harmonious to the ear;
> Heaven with the echo shall resound,
> And all the earth shall hear.
>
> Grace first contrived a way
> To save rebellious man;
> And all the steps that grace display,
> Which drew the wondrous plan.

Grace first inscribed my name
In God's eternal book;
'Twas grace that gave me to the Lamb,
Who all my sorrows took.

Grace turned my wandering feet
To tread the heavenly road;
And new supplies each hour I meet,
While pressing on to God.

Grace taught my soul to pray,
And made my eyes o'erflow;
'Tis grace that kept me to this day,
And will not let me go.

Grace all the work shall crown,
Through everlasting days;
It lays in heaven the topmost stone,
And well deserves the praise.[39]

'The grace of the Lord Jesus be with God's people. Amen.'

Appendices

Appendix 1
The Christology of Revelation

Christology is the theological name by which we describe the biblical doctrine of the person and work of the Lord Jesus Christ. At the very beginning of our exposition we saw that the whole of the Bible is full of Christ, and that what is true of Scripture as a whole is especially and gloriously true of this final portion of God's Word — the book of Revelation. It is Christ's revelation or manifestation or unveiling of Himself. That is why we should never refer to the book as 'the Revelation of John', for that is completely incorrect. It is the revelation of Christ, by Christ to John and so to us. That makes all the difference!

In this note, it is worth gathering together the titles of Christ that occur in the book and meditating upon each one of them carefully in our minds and hearts. One writer comments, 'The very name of the book of Revelation means that its content is intended to be a disclosure of the Person of Christ. He is not incidental to its action: He is its chief subject. Even in those chapters where signs and symbols seem uppermost and where the cataclysmic judgements of God eclipse all other interests, the Person of Christ is still central.'[40]

Start by reading again the following passages: chapters 1:12–18; 5:5–12; 14:14–16, 19:11–16. If we had to settle for just two titles or descriptions of Christ, then they would surely be Christ 'the Lamb' and Christ 'the King of kings and Lord of lords'. But the whole list is very much longer!

The faithful witness (1:5)
The firstborn from the dead (1:5)
The ruler of the kings of the earth (1:5)

209

Him who loves us and has freed us from our sins by
his blood (1:5)

The Living One (1:18)

The One who holds 'the keys of death and Hades' (1:18)

Him who holds the seven stars in his right hand and
walks among the seven golden lampstands (2:1)

The Lion of the tribe of Judah (5:5)

The Root of David (5:5)

A Lamb, looking as if it had been slain (5:6)

The Lamb that was slain from the creation of the world
(13:8)

Faithful and True (19:11)

The Word of God (19:13)

The King of kings and Lord of lords (19:16)

The Alpha and the Omega (22:13)

The First and the Last (22:13)

The Beginning and the End (22:13)

The Root and Offspring of David (22:16)

The bright Morning Star (22:16)

The One who says, 'Yes, I am coming soon.' (22:20)

To which we chorus in response, 'Amen. Come, Lord Jesus.'

Appendix 2
What do others teach about the millennium?

'So much has been said or written about these thousand years, out of all proportion to the very little that is said about them in the Bible.'[41]

In chapter 18 of this book I sought to open up the main lines of the teaching in Revelation 20 concerning the millennium. As I said then, the word itself means 'a period of one thousand years'. Such a period is referred to in every verse from verse 2 to verse 7 inclusive. My exposition, although I did not say so at the time, amounted to what is known historically as the *a-millennial* (or *non-millennial*) interpretation, which I believe to be the right and true exposition which Scripture requires.

But that is not the only interpretation of Revelation 20 which has been offered at different times. Many Christ-honouring and Bible-loving believers have felt the passage demands another interpretation. Indeed two other main lines of interpretation have been advanced, and have become known as the *post-millennial* and the *pre-millennial* interpretations. In my view (and that of other, better men!), they are seriously wrong at many points, but it is important to urge that the hot and sometimes even vindictive passions that have been aroused over this subject are most grievous in their dishonouring of the Saviour and the gospel. Some friends, whatever interpretation they may have taken, have made the serious mistake of putting the millennium 'centre-stage' in their whole doctrinal system, making it a test of fellowship or orthodoxy among Christians, and sometimes virtually un-Christianizing or unchurching brothers and sisters in Christ who genuinely understand these matters differently. So a note of caution needs to be sounded concerning the whole spirit or manner in which we contend for the truth. We need, as someone has said, not only the doctrines of grace but the grace of the doctrines!

A-millennialism

The essence of a-millennialism, as we have seen, is that the thousand years are a symbolic picture of the whole period from the first to the second coming of the Lord Jesus Christ. In other words, we are living in the millennium right now.

In chapter 20:1—3 this period is viewed from the earth, while in chapter 20:4—6 it is viewed in heaven. There follows Satan's little season (20:7—9), and Christ's return leading to the final discomfiting and destruction of the devil (20: 9—10), thus setting the stage for the final judgement to be in session (20:11—15). Among Bible students who have maintained this position are William Hendriksen and W. J. Grier.[42]

Post-millennialism

This interpretation teaches that at the end of what it calls the gospel dispensation there will be a millennial period (whether literal or symbolic they would disagree among themselves) when Christianity will prevail upon the earth — a sort of 'Golden Age' of immense gospel blessing and gospel advance, with the result that a largely converted world will be waiting to greet the Lord Jesus Christ at His appearing.

But surely the Bible does not hold out the prospect of such a largely converted world when Christ comes again — very much the opposite! Yet choice men like John Bunyan and B. B. Warfield have cherished this interpretation.

Pre-millennialism

As the use of 'pre-' implies, these friends believe that Christ's second coming will introduce the millennium rather than follow it. After the battle of Armageddon, Christ will come and reign literally at Jerusalem, with the restoration of the temple worship and the sacrificial system. The godly Scottish minister Andrew Bonar held to this view, as does Merrill C. Tenney in our own day.

But it presents a host of problems. The Revelation 20 passage makes no reference whatsoever to the Jews, an earthly or national kingdom or the land of Palestine. What is more, the literal rebuilding of the Jerusalem temple and the literal re-establishing of the Old Testament sacrificial system would be 'the most daring denial of the all-sufficiency of the sacrifice of Christ, and of the efficacy of the blood of His atonement'.[43] It would surely be a step backwards from light into darkness, from fulfilment back to type. And this interpretation imports the whole unscriptural notion of the 'secret rapture' of believers, which requires an interim secret coming of the Lord Jesus Christ between His first coming proper and His second coming proper.

Appendix 3
A note on books

Multitudes of commentaries, expositions and studies arising out of the book of Revelation have been published over the years, and it is easy to become confused as to which are reliable guides and which are not. So here is a short list of pointers for the further study of Revelation, each of them to be recommended.

William Hendriksen's *More than Conquerors* is justly famous, and an absolute necessity for the Bible student. And every Christian should be a Bible student! My own understanding of Revelation, since I began studying it seriously back in 1972, owes more to Dr Hendriksen's book than to any other single volume. It is currently published by Baker and distributed through Evangelical Press.

Geoffrey Wilson has written on *Revelation*, and this paperback from Evangelical Press came out just in time to help me write this book! Like his other New Testament commentaries, it is consistently helpful and reliable, going through each chapter carefully, verse by verse.

How are you with big books? One to be very highly recommended is Herman Hoeksema's *Behold He Cometh* — a big 726-pager from Reformed Free Publishing Association. It is magnificent! If you feel you can eventually proceed to this one, please do!

Of the other books already mentioned via the references, I would draw your attention to the commentary on *Revelation* by James Beverlin Ramsey in the Geneva Series of Commentaries from the Banner of Truth. This covers only chapters 1—11, but is of rich spiritual worth, especially in its exposition of the letters of chapters 2 and 3 and the visions of heaven in chapters 4 and 5.

So go to it!

References

1. James Laing's moving story is told in 'Another Lily Gathered', to be found in *Memoir and Remains of Robert Murray M'Cheyne*, by Andrew Bonar, Banner of Truth.
2. References to Hendriksen are to William Hendriksen, *More Than Conquerors*, currently published by Baker (though mine is an earlier Tyndale Press edition).
3. William Still, *And I Saw . . .* Didasko Press, p. 14. All references to Still are to this commentary.
4. Merrill C. Tenney, *Interpreting Revelation*, Pickering and Inglis, p. 48.
5. James Beverlin Ramsey, *Revelation*, Banner of Truth, p. 55.
6. A clear summary of the preterist, historicist, futurist and idealist views may be found in Leon Morris, *Revelation*, Tyndale Press, pp. 16—18.
7. Taken from Fred Mitchell, *The Lamb Upon His Throne*, Marshall, Morgan and Scott, p. 46. These were the Keswick Convention Bible Readings for 1951. This style of interpretation, though dividing up the periods of church history differently, is also followed by Basil F. C. Atkinson, *The War Against Satan*, Protestant Truth Society.
8. Octavius Winslow, *Personal Declension and Revival of Religion in the Soul*, Banner of Truth, ch. 2.
9. Geoffrey B. Wilson, *Revelation*, Evangelical Press, p. 31. All references to Wilson are to this commentary.
10. Read the moving account of the martyrdom of Polycarp, Bishop of Smyrna, in Hendriksen, *More Than Conquerors*, p. 64.
11. Hugh D. Morgan, *The Holiness of God and of His People*, Evangelical Press of Wales, p. 5.
12. R. J. Graham, *Christ and His Churches*, Sovereign Grace Union, p. 27.
13. Ramsey, *Revelation*, pp. 177f.
14. See John Flavel's sermons on Revelation 3:20 in *Works, Vol. 4*, Banner of Truth. Flavel (one of my favourite Puritans!) incorporates and develops an evangelistic use of the text, but he makes a right evangelistic use, with the emphasis upon God's power and grace and the sinner's impotence and inability, in contrast with the wrong and weak evangelistic use made of the

verse by much contemporary evangelism. Consider some of the divisions of his material: 'Jesus Christ an earnest Suitor for union and communion with the souls of sinners; Jesus Christ will not refuse to come in to the soul of the vilest sinner when it is made willing to open to Him; No man's soul will savingly and effectually open to receive Christ until the quickening voice of Christ be first heard in the soul.' And he goes on to give a rich and satisfying exposition of the communion with Christ emphasis of the text.

15.   Ramsey, *Revelation*, p. 225.
16.   This section of application owes much to a fine portion in Ramsey, *Revelation*, pp. 292—294.
17.   C. H. Spurgeon, *Metropolitan Tabernacle Pulpit, Vol. 21*, Pilgrim Publications, p. 174.
18.   Herman Hoeksema, *Behold He Cometh*, Reformed Free Publishing Association, p. 236. All references to Hoeksema are to this commentary.
19.   Ramsey, *Revelation*, p. 325.
20.   *Hymns for the Waiting Church*, no. 883. The hymn book was published in Birmingham in 1882.
21.   Guy Appéré, *Dialogue With God*, Evangelical Press, chapter 1.
22.   Wilson, *Revelation*, p. 80.
23.   Still, *And I Saw*, p. 57.
24.   Morris, *Revelation*, p. 142.
25.   Hoeksema, *Behold He Cometh!*, p. 369.
26.   This is demonstrated excellently by Hendriksen, *More Than Conquerors*, pp. 137—140.
27.   Quoted in *Banner of Truth* Magazine, Issue 251—2, Aug—Sept. 1984, p. 61.
28.   Thomas Brooks, *Precious Remedies Against Satan's Devices*, Banner of Truth — available separately in paperback, or in *Works, Vol. 1*.
29.   J. I. Packer, *Knowing God*, Hodder and Stoughton, p. 135.
30.   A. W. Pink, *The Attributes of God*, Baker, p. 185.
31.   Quoted from Iain H. Murray, *The Life of Arthur W. Pink*, Banner of Truth, p. 182.
32.   For fuller details, see the description in Hendriksen, *More Than Conquerors*, p. 179f.
33.   Charles Bradley, quoted by C. H. Spurgeon in *My Sermon Notes, Vol. 4*, Baker, p. 397.
34.   Wilson, *Revelation*, p. 172.
35.   Jock Purves, *Fair Sunshine*, Banner of Truth, p. 120.
36.   Wilson, *Revelation*, p. 176.
37.   Wilson, *Revelation*, p. 180.
38.   J. I. Packer, *God Has Spoken*, Hodder and Stoughton. A fine and very readable treatment of the whole issue of the inspiration and authority of the Bible is Brian H. Edwards, *Nothing But The Truth*, Evangelical Press.
39.   Try singing it sometime to the tune *Cranbrook*!

40. Tenney, *Interpreting Revelation*, p. 117. He observes further down the same page that 'This Christological emphasis is one of the most important keys to Revelation. By beginning with the Person as the chief interpretative factor, fruitless debate over details can be minimized, and the main purpose of the book can be kept constantly in sight.' We may say a hearty 'Amen!' to that! Tenney divides the book Christologically like this: Christ in communication (1:1–8); Christ in the church (1:9–3:22); Christ in the cosmos (4:1–16:21); Christ in conquest (17:1–21:8); Christ in consummation (21:9–22:5); and Christ challenging (22:6–21).

41. Someone wrote that somewhere – but I cannot remember who or where!

42. William Hendriksen, *The Bible on the Life Hereafter.* Baker, contains an excellent summary of this interpretation (pp. 150–156). Chapter 2 of W. J. Grier, *The Momentous Event*, Banner of Truth, gives a most succinct summary of the a-millennial position and then explains most helpfully the difficulties and objections inherent in the other two interpretations (pp. 13–17). Also worth consulting is Louis Berkhof, *Systematic Theology*, Banner of Truth, pp. 708–719.

43. A statement quoted in Grier, *Momentous Event*, p. 38.